ALTONA BROWN

Ruby

ALTONA BROWN

Ruby

SPIRIT MOUNTAIN PRESS
P.O. BOX 1214 FAIRBANKS, ALASKA 99707

ISBN: 0-910871-06-X

Interviewing and Editing:
Yvonne Yarber and Curt Madison

Photography:
Curt Madison (unless otherwise noted)

Translations:
Eliza Jones (her translations in the text are followed by the initials E.J.) Courtesy of the Alaska Native Language Center, University of Alaska-Fairbanks.

Material collected June 1980 in Ruby, Alaska and April 1982 Fairbanks, Alaska.

Manuscript approved by Altona Brown, 1983.

SPIRIT MOUNTAIN PRESS
P.O. BOX 1214 FAIRBANKS, ALASKA 99707

Produced and Funded by:
Yukon-Koyukuk School District of Alaska

Regional School Board:
Donald Honea Sr. - Chairman
Pat McCarty - Vice Chairman
Eddie Bergman - Treasurer
Fred Lee Bifelt - Clerk
Luke Titus

Superintendent: Joe Cooper
Assistant superintendent: Fred Lau
Project Coordinator: Don Kratzer

Supplemental funding:
Johnson O'Malley Grant - EOOC14202516

**Library of Congress
Cataloging in Publication Data**

Madison, Curt
Yarber, Yvonne
Brown, Altona - Ruby. A Biography
YKSD Biography Series
ISBN 0-910871-06-X

1. Brown, Altona 2. Koyukon-Athabaskan
3. Alaska Biography

Cover Photo:
Altona Brown with her .22 Special on the road past Long Creek, June 1980.

Frontispiece:
Altona Brown with her grandson Claude Keough on her front porch in Ruby, June 1980.

A Note From a Linguist

As you read through this autobiography you will notice a style and a diction you may not have seen before in print. This is because it is an oral storytelling style. This autobiography has been compiled from many hours of taped interviews. As you read you should listen for the sound of the spoken voice. While it has not been possible to show all the rhythms and nuances of the speaker's voice, much of the original style has been kept. If posssible you should read aloud and use your knowledge of the way the old people speak to recapture the style of the original.

This autobiography has been written in the original style for three reasons. First, the original style is a kind of dramatic poetry that depends on pacing, succinctness, and semantic indirectness for its narrative impact. The original diction is part and parcel of its message and the editors have kept that diction out of a deep respect for the person represented in this autobiography.

The second reason for keeping the original diction is that it gives a good example of some of the varied richness of the English language. English as it is spoken in many parts of the world and by many different people varies in style and the editors feel that it is important for you as a reader to know, understand and respect the wide resources of this variation in English.

The third reason for writing in the original style is that this style will be familiar to many of you who will read this book. The editors hope that you will enjoy reading something in a style that you may never have seen written before even though you have heard it spoken many times.

Ron Scollon
Alaska Native Language Center
University of Alaska
Fairbanks
1979

Acknowledgements

Our thanks to the many people who have helped with this book: Marie Hunter and Claude Keough for hospitality and support; Jim and Beth Ehrhart for a warm house, food, and conversation; the Ruby school staff for logistical support; Gladys Dart for introducing us to Altona and beginning work with her; Renee Blahuta of the University of Alaska Archives in Fairbanks for assistance; Eliza Jones of the Alaska Native Language Center for translations, advice and moral support; Ron Scollon for his Note From a Linguist; Bea Hagen for typing transcripts; Cheryl DeHart for manuscript typing; Liza Vernet for her proofreading expertise.

Additional thanks to the Yukon-Koyukuk School District people; Bob Maguire who created this project before leaving YKSD for other adventures; Mavis Brown, Fred Lau and Joe Cooper for all the administrative red tape unravelled; and the Regional School Board who consider local curriculum a top priority and support it with the necessary funds.

Finally, appreciation goes to the folks at Spirit Mountain Press who do all the work required of a publishing staff; Eva Bee for typesetting and proofing; Judy Morris, jack-of-all-trades in training, Doug Miller for his artistic touch in layout; and Larry Laraby, the head man and sitting duck.

Tape recording over tea at the Ehrhart's home in Ruby, 1980. L-r: Curt Madison, Jim Ehrhart, Beth Ehrhart, Yvonne Yarber, Altona Brown.

All royalties from the sale of this book go to the Yukon-Koyukuk School District for the production of more autobiographies.

This is the first printing of this book. Please let us know about any corrections for future printings.

Foreword

This book is the fourteenth produced by the Yukon-Koyukuk School District in a series meant to provide cultural understanding of our own area and relevant role models for students. Too often Interior Alaska is ignored in books or mentioned only in conjunction with its mineral resources such as the gold rush or oil pipeline. We are gauged by what we are worth to Outside people. People living in the Interior certainly have been affected by those things but also by missionaries, wage labor, fur prices, celebrations, spring hunts, schools, technology, potlatches, and much more. For residents, Interior Alaska is all of those things people do together, whether in the woods, on the river, in the village or on Two Street. It's a rich and varied culture often glossed over in favor of things more easily written and understood.

This project was begun in 1977 by Bob Maguire. Representatives of Indian Education Parent Committees from each of Yukon-Koyukuk School District's eleven villages met in Fairbanks February of 1978 to choose two people from each village to write about. A variety of selection means were used—from school committees to village council elections. Despite the fact that most of the representatives were women, few women were chosen for the books. As the years passed, more women were added to give a more complete accounting of recent cultural changes.

It is our goal to provide a vehicle for people who live around us so they can describe the events of their lives in their own words. To be singled out as an individual as we have done in this series has not always been comfortable for the biographees, particularly for those who carry the strong Koyukon value of being humble. Talking about oneself has been a conflict overridden by the desire and overwhelming need to give young people some understanding of their own history in a form they have become accustomed to. A growing number of elders who can't read or write themselves think young people won't believe anything unless it's written in a book. This project attempts to give oral knowledge equal time in the schools.

As materials of this kind become more common, methods of gathering and presenting oral history get better. The most important ingredient is trust. After many hours of interview, people often relax to the point of saying some personal things they prefer left unpublished. After editing the tape transcripts we bring the rough draft manuscript back to the biographees to let them add or delete things before it becomes public. Too often those of us living in rural Alaska have been researched *on* or written *about* for an audience far away. This series is meant to bring information full round--from us back to us for our own uses.

Too many people in the Interior have felt ripped-off by journalists and bureaucrats. Hundreds pass through every year, all wanting information and many never to return. Occasionally their finished work may find its way back to the source only to flare emotions when people feel misrepresented. Perhaps a tight deadline or the lack of travel money may be the excuse for not returning for verification or approval. That is no consolation for the people who opened up and shared something of themselves and are left feeling betrayed. We work closely with the biographees to check facts and intentions. The books need to be intimate and daring but the last thing we want to do is make someone's life more difficult. We need to share information in a wholesome way. After all, we're all in this together.

Comments about the biographies, their use, corrections, questions, or anything else is welcome.

Curt Madison
Yvonne Yarber
December 10, 1982
Manley Hot Springs
Alaska 99756

Table of Contents

A Note From a Linguist	5
Acknowledgements	6
Foreword	7
Table of Contents	8
Introduction	9
Glossary	10
Maps	11

CHAPTER ONE — OLDER PEOPLE

Tough Little Woman	12
Born	14
Sleep with Dried Up Old Woman	18
Up the Hill	20
Potlatch at Louden with Grandma Bogie	21
Lewis Landing	23
Nughutlagheelinh Dinh	27
1911	29
Eight Mile	32
Medicine People	34
Frogs	36
School	38
Grandmother	41

CHAPTER TWO — FANTASTIC STORY

First White People	44
Starvation	48

CHAPTER THREE — POLIO

Polio	53

CHAPTER FOUR — TWELVE AND MARRIED

Sakkonh gheeltonee	60
My Baby Dies	66

CHAPTER FIVE — BEARS

Women and Bears	69
Go Listen for Something	70
Killing Bear in Hole with Madeline	73
Papa's Words	82

CHAPTER SIX — LIFE WITH DAGO KID

Seventeen Years Old	84
Enjoying Work	91
Cutting Fish	94
Deliver Babies	98
Trapping	99
Food on the Trapline	103
Gambling	108

CHAPTER SEVEN — ALTONA ON HER OWN

Raising Kids	110
Sewing	113
Hunting with Dolly	114

CHAPTER EIGHT — YUKI LAKE ALONE

Tamarack My Friend	118
Index	127
Family Tree	128

Introduction

Altona Brown was born in 1904 into the midst of gold rush fever. Miners moved in hoardes from the Klondike to Fairbanks to the Innoko to Ruby. Steamboats churned the Middle Yukon in a frenzy to get the gold. But before the miners were the Natives and after the miners left the Natives remained.

Altona has learned to live with change. The hardships she endured have left their mark on her tough but resilient character. As a young girl she overcame polio. As an elder her strong heart has already worn out several pacemakers.

Her ancestors were noted medicine people and many people think the knowledge was passed on. She exudes a powerful presence. As an example, twice she has broken her arm and set it herself. The first time was on the trapline as a young woman, the second only a few years ago near the Ruby airport while out checking rabbit snares. The second break was in the forearm. She went back to her sled, got her poleax and kneeled down with the handle behind her knees. Clasping the broken arm to the handle with her good hand she leaned back and twisted until the bones "sounded right". A few days later a visitor insisted she go to a doctor for an x-ray. There was nothing they could do — the set was perfect.

Although she will still compose Indian songs and sew, her 80 years have slowed her down a bit. She no longer cuts 120 salmon an hour taking out the back bones, slicing the fillets and flinging them on-to the rack. But she dug her own 12 foot deep cesspool by hand last year, got her own smokehouse wood, and drove her boat and snowmachine.

Altona Brown is the living connection with another era, tough and quite amazing.

Glossary

aabaa - Koyukon exclamation of pain; ouch!

baasee' - Koyukon word meaning thank-you.

hutłanee - Koyukon, Athabaskan word meaning taboo or bad luck sign (E.J.)

Kokrines - a large Athabaskan village in the early 1900's, located twenty-seven miles northeast of Ruby on the Yukon River. References to this village are made in the writings of Father Jette. Many of the residents later moved to Ruby, leaving Kokrines unpopulated except for an occasional trapper or summer resident.

Louden - former Athabaskan settlement on the Yukon River, 43 miles east of Nulato (64°38'N, 156°41'W). The 1890 census recorded a population of 39. In 1903 the U.S. Army Signal Corps established a telegraph station. The people of Louden later moved to the more populated villages of Galena and Ruby leaving Louden uninhabited.

Melozi Station - former Athabaskan settlement located at the mouth of the Melozitna River and reported by Petroff to have a population of 30 in 1880. It later became a telegraph station and riverboat landing.

romaine - babiche; moose or caribou rawhide rope.

Ruby - a village on the Yukon River which began as a port and supply center when gold was found at Long Creek in 1911. Although the population was predominately non-Native many Athabaskans moved from Louden and Kokrines to Ruby where they found work or a market for fish, sleds, snowshoes, firewood, sewing and furs. During it's early years the population was over 1,000 dropping to 128 by 1920. Ruby is now an incorporated second class city and Native village under the Alaska Native Land Claims Act. Present population is close to 225; about 35 being non-Native. Services and facilities include an elementary and high school, airfield, television, telephone, health clinic, sawmill, bulk fuel plant, laundromat, and community center. Goldmining continues in outlying areas.

sodaa - Koyukon word used when addressing an older sister (E.J.)

tłabaas - the Koyukon name for the curved knife used to cut fish; often made out of old carpenter saw blades.

Mabel Charlie, Altona Brown and Ralph Perdue in Fairbanks at the 1969 FNA potlatch. "They want me to sing for those five people that drowned down river."

Local Area

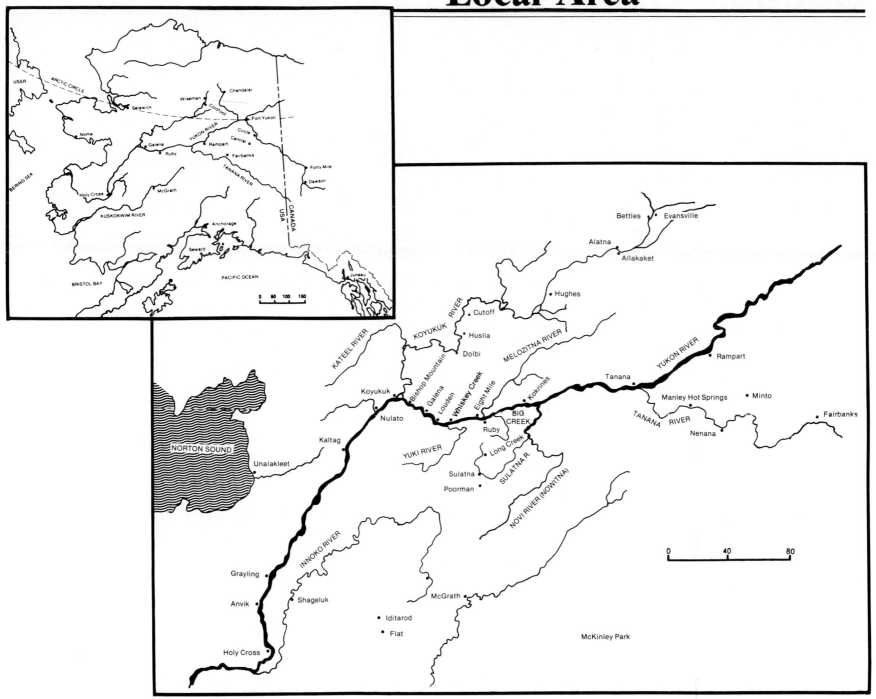

Chapter One: Older People

Tough Little Woman

Here was Papa's mother with a whole bunch of kids and Papa's father brought home two or three womens. I don't know if this was at Kateel or Dolbi. It was up there someplace. That's where their home used to be. Those people those days never used to have a home. Oh, they have villages but they very seldom come to the villages — just for the doing, meeting or potlatch, something like that. They're all the time going with the animal. They follow the animal around to eat and that's when he got these three womens. That's how come we're related all the way up to Tanana with close relatives. They must have been nice looking guys because they had girlfriends all over and had babies everywhere. Papa's papa and all his brothers, big tall guys. I know one of them was *Taayinaadliyo*, another one was *Laaleeghona* and the younger one was *Dilogh HɯdaatIggunh*. He was the fastest runner! Wintertime they put dry birch wood shavings in their mouth when they run. Between their teeth to catch the frost. And always hold a piece of wood in their hand to hold the sweat. There's about seven of them.

So Papa's mother moved out. She took her kids and moved down the river. They said she had seven boys and some girls. Some of them grown up already. Papa was the youngest one. He was still so much baby. I guess he remembers though when they moved down to where they call *Hɯnoogha Dinh*, up from mouth of Koyukuk River. She made a dugout living quarters there. She was tough. They said she was small woman, but strong. *Kk'okkanaa* was her name. There must be some reason why they called her that. She was blind at the end. Burned to death sitting next to the fire when everybody ran off after willow grouse. (*Kkanaa* means "conversation, speech or language." The name was probably longer originally meaning something like good speaker. Often people would drop half of a long name and use a shortened version. E.J.)

Papa was small but he remembers well that she would make romaine and use that to snare caribou with. He was too small to go with her and would stay home all day with his old aunt. She was so stingy she never give him nothing to eat all day. He would wait for his mamma to come home to feed him. He used to put his mamma's caribou mitts on his feet to go out to the bank and look for his mom. He had one great big dog with flopped-ear named *K'its'ahonokkaagha*. Papa would say, "*K'its'ahonokkaagha*, how far Mom is coming?" If his mom is not close to the camp then the dog just put his head down, never say nothing. But if his mom is close that red dog wag his tail. He used to talk to this dog all the time. The dog took care of him.

When his mother killed caribou with snare she made a big long fence with trees. Well, dropping trees, that's not very easy those days. They didn't have no crosscut saw, only stone ax. But I guess stone ax was just as good. They don't need big logs for their house. Very little timber they need for dugout house in the ground. They put poles over it and then they bank it up. Birch bark then moss and cover it up with dirt. They have hole in the middle. I never seen one. Mary Dean told me that she seen one in Louden. Then they have a fire right in the middle. They cover it up, bank it up before they go to bed. That's hot all night. And in the morning they uncover it and the coals are still there to start their fire again.

This one time his aunt took him to where his mother put out snares for the caribou. She made a fence all the way across the small valley. He saw his mom was killing the caribou with the spear. Big long pole. Special spear they used to use. She just poked him in the stomach from the back

13

and just keep poking it till it keel over. Then she take it out of the snare and butcher it up. Tough little woman.

I don't know what kind of a knife you call what she butcher it with. From those black stones he said. They were sharp like a razor. When Papa was getting a little bigger they had a knife with a bone handle that's been made someplace. There was some traders. Kobuk people had first contact with Russians, they had the knife and ax and gun. The first gun Papa ever seen had copper barrel with one shell. He said those shell was just like marbles and they put them in something that had a little powder thing on it and some kind of caps. Oh, I don't know how it was, I know they had to pay lots for those things.

Papa says his mom used to make him rabbit skin suit. She tan it and make strips and roll it. Then she just crochet that suit for him. He wear that all winter. Pants and the tops. Two pieces. I guess he couldn't be wearing one piece because he'd grow out of it in one winter. About the middle of winter he put it inside out when the fur start to wear off one side of it. By the spring time both sides was hardly any hair on it. Only between the knitted part. So he wear it all summer. Next fall it's just below his knees sometimes before he get a new suit! When us kids got tired of wearing same clothes all the time he would tell us about this rabbit skin.

Born

The girl he ran away from was his cousin. My father Big Joe. They tried to make him marry his cousin in Koyukuk so he jumped on the boat, a sternwheeler, and went to Bettles. It was about the first boat going up the Koyukuk River for miners. Just a kid. Teenager. But he was a big man. Other big people around here then called Big William, Big Bob, and Big Albert. They all got jobs packing supplies for miners.

"That's my mom. Must be 1910 because she was carrying my brother."

Big Albert with his father Hardluck in the back. Kokrines circa 1914. Photo by Jette.

After that he worked in Dawson. Then he went to Circle and overland to Central. That's where he had a girlfriend, older woman. I don't know her name. Those big guys was just like the military fooling around with all kinds of womens. That's how we're related all up the river. Papa went from Central to Forty Mile and right away to Fairbanks when everybody rushed there. One summer he worked around Fairbanks and Chena but next spring he got homesick so he got on a boat and came on down to the mouth of the Koyukuk.

That fall he met my mother. She was already given away to another man that was supposed to be her husband but Big Joe and her got together and took off. His Indian name is *K'akk'aadodeedaah*, the sound a brown bear makes when they kill him. *Aadodeedaah* is the part they take for the name of children. The "*daah*" part means "sound".

January 4, 1904, I was born. Mom was carrying me when they went up the Novi in the fall. They go up by boat and stay all winter. But Big Joe brought her down to her aunt, Mrs. Phillip, so I could be born. They stayed at the point below Kokrines. About four miles below the village.

Altogether they had sixteen children. Most of them died right away. Some got to walk, some got older, and now only three are left. Me, the oldest sister Rose, and youngest brother Rocker.

The first thing I remember I was with Cecelia Williams and Uncle Williams. They adopted me down Nulato. Madeline Solomon was adopted by them the same time. That's why we call each other sister. They must have had me two years or more. Until I was big enough to know what they were doing. They were fighting lots. Everytime they fought or they talk rough language I'd faint. As soon as they started using big words and shout at one another I pass out.

Old Man Stickman and my real Papa were good friends. He sent word upriver to my Papa to come down and get me. He thought I might not come to one of those times. Just here and there I remember. Coming upriver Papa put up a big sail in the boat. And a little above Koyukuk it got rough so we landed. There was a smokehouse there, fish camp, I guess. We stayed a little while and left, I don't remember much.

I didn't find out Cecelia wasn't my mother till I was nine years old. Nine years old is when my real parents take me back. Everytime Papa and Mom say anything to me, scold me, I cry for Cecelia and Uncle William. All the time until I was nine, I thought they were my real people. Not until after Uncle William died did I find out they weren't my folks. Uncle William was Mama's first cousin. Finally I got old enough to understand. My brother explained to me who my real Papa was.

From Nulato, next time I remember we were staying above Whiskey Creek right where Sidney Huntington has a fish camp now. *Noosa Ghunh* is the name of the place. Right abreast of the big island. We lived there a long time. My aunty and her husband Gurtler were living up in the slough. Near Little Creek. Their cache uprights are still there with tin nailed to them.

Lot of aunties around then. Mom was walking over to the smokehouse and told me to go over to aunty. She called me and I walked over to her. There was a puppy behind the tent. It was hot and lot of bugs. She had to burn some punk. That stuff off the birch tree. Those big hard ones. She was burning that on the outside of the tent. It keeps all the flies and all the bugs away. Aunty was lying down. I don't know when her husband died. I wasn't born yet. She was married to my Mama's uncle. Her father's brother, oldest brother. I never knew him, but I guess his name was Pitka. I didn't know their Indian name. They were big medicine people and you weren't supposed to call them by name in Indian.

I was going over there and my aunty was lying down. Frank, her crippled son, was sleeping. "*Kkaa'*" she said, "Don't go near that fire!" And those punks burn just like coal. It never go out. Once it gets to burn, well, it just burns. And it's red hot. Stinks though, this punk. So I went over there and I don't like the smell of it. I want Mama to put mosquito net on the bank. That's what I was crying about. And aunty said, "*Haa*, there's man coming. And that man is wounded one. And he gets awfully mad." They used to tell me such a story because I cry too much.

So, anyway, I went in her tent and she says, "*Kkaa*'! Don't go near that fire!" Frank was sleeping so I quit crying. And just at that time, the puppy was lying behind the tent. Lying down in the shade. He was scratching and singing like a whine, "Unn, unn, unn."

My aunt just got mad and gee, she was a little woman. She jumped up and I see that picture for the longest time. She went out there and just hit him over head with ax! Killed it. Just because he make that noise. Scratching himself, "unnn, unnn, unnn."

I got scared. I remember I got scared and I run over to my other aunt. My papa's oldest brother's wife, *Kk'ohunaa'oh*. She was the mother to Cheechako John. Big woman. Great big woman. She was a nice looking woman, but she was sick all the time. I run over there. She said, "What you're doing?"

"My aunty killed a dog." And I started crying again.

Sleep With Dried Up Old Woman

I was in bed. I sleep with my aunt, my father's oldest sister, *Neeldokkokk'a* and I always put my hand around her neck or around her breast and sleep that way. Since my mom had a baby at that time. It died afterwards. So I couldn't do that. I couldn't sleep with her. So I sleep with my aunt.

Sleeping. And here I was going to put my hand up to her, around her neck and . . . skinny! I jumped up! Looked at her. It was different woman! Old woman I was sleeping with. Old, dried up woman! I started to cry. It was my papa's aunt. Old woman. She stayed with us for a long time. She's buried down there at Eight Mile on the other side. She lived with us for a long, long time. And she got up. Holding me and she was trying to sing to me and everything. You know how old ladies does. Nope, I wouldn't quit. She got up and got some prunes for me and a drink of water. Tried to do everything nice for me. But no, I cried.

All of a sudden my aunt came back. Here she went up the slough. Up to Gurtler's camp. Homestead. And deliver a baby. That's why this old lady come over from next door and stayed with me. I guess I was sleeping when Gurtler came down and got her to go deliver the baby.

So from there I wouldn't sleep. I just wouldn't sleep. I watch her. I don't know where my folks was. They were out trapping I guess. And they took Rose with them because Rose wouldn't mind anybody. They left me home 'cause I got sick for nothing. I wouldn't sleep and that next day she was going up again and she had to pack me on her back.

My Aunt Aggie Gurtler was in bed. I was wonder why she was in bed? It made me feel bad. I started crying again. Then

"Dorothy Abraham, our great-aunt. Her husband was John Abraham. I know she was cripple for seven years and sat like that."

she showed me the baby that my aunt found. Alfred Gurtler and his brother were there. This is the third one they had. That was born. But she didn't tell me how it was born. Aunt Aggie said my Aunt found it up where uncle was cutting wood. They always told us they find babies under tree. I believed it. We never seen them. We don't know any better. We seen woman with big stomach alright, but Mamma said they were sick. We didn't know there was baby in there.

We started to go but I wouldn't go. I thought the baby should belong to my aunt. She should take it home. She found it! It must belong to her. They said everything to me until I made up my mind she was going to pack me home.

Up the Hill

My aunt took me up the hill. We got some big hills back there. She took me way up the hill. It was in falltime. She packed me up on her back. I start to sing away. Good weather and this fresh snow you see the tracks and see the chickadees on the trees. I start to sing away. Then she just shift her shoulder and I fell in the snow. She walked away. She say, "You stay here till I get back."

I stayed there long time rolling around in the snow. She was gone a long time. I must have slept. But I was warm. I had fur parka, muskrat parka with fur in and fur out. And then I had caribou fawn-skin pants with boots sewed to it. Toasty warm. And the mitts is sewed onto the sleeves so no snow get in there.

When she was coming back I got scared of her. I hear her crying. I was wondering what she was crying about. And here I cry for nothing all the time. I never think nothing of it. She was crying and walking in snowshoes. I crawled under a tree. Big tree was there. I crawled under there and hide away from her. "Okay," she thought, "Okay, if you're going to hide just go ahead and hide." She must have seen me, but she just walked by going down the hill. I stayed there. I must have slept, 'cause pretty soon she come. Woke me up.

"Did you get scared?" she said. I said, "No. From what?" Then she packed me home. I guess she packed all her animals home first as long as I was warm. Then she came back. She was trapping. I never seen her trap. Only one time, I thought maybe that was her trap.

It was a pile of sticks and she was pulling marten out of there. Pile of sticks. She didn't have a steel trap. So I don't know. The pile of sticks was all scattered. After she pull that marten out of there, well, she was fooling around for a long time. She told me just stay on the trail. So I didn't watch her. I thought maybe she didn't want me to watch her, I guess. I stayed on the trail. I was scared of that marten. I didn't want to monkey with it.

Her husband had died not very long before that. And her two boys. She lost her two teenaged boys and all she had. She didn't have very many kids. I don't know if that's all she had, but that's all she had with her when her husband died suddenly. Her eyes were sore all the time from crying. She didn't get married right away. She was fussy. She worked hard and when she finally got a man she wanted, well, she married him and they had these two boys. Maybe she had more, but then I don't think so. And she lost her husband and shortly afterwards these two boys.

Potlatch at Louden with Grandma Bogie

Long time ago when they have potlatch it lasts couple weeks, three weeks maybe sometime. It lasts. They sing and dance, carry on. That's memorial potlatch. They don't just come in and throw everything down and leave. No. That's the way they put away their people. When they make memorial potlatch they put away the person. That's the main thing. After they do that, they give them up. Give them up and they figure the spirit isn't around there anymore.

They used to moan over those people so much. They dance, sing, make songs. Every evening. And during the day they'd go out and hunt. Cook that up and feed everybody for two or three weeks. I guess that's what

Midnight lunch at a Kokrines potlatch, circa 1910-1915. l-r: 1. baby Anik Yaska, held by 2. Margaret Charles 3. Harry Jones 4. Mrs. Big John 5. Henry Pilot 6. unidentified 7. Basel Peters 8. Mrs. Mary Ivan 9. Jenny Thompson 10. unidentified 11. Mrs. Slim Dick with child 12. Johnny Glass

they were doing when we were in Louden. Then Papa got mad about something. He hooked up the dogs. Mamma talked to him. He wouldn't say nothing. He wouldn't answer. He was the kind of man that never talked much. Quiet. He hooked up and took me home. I was sick for two days. It was something I ate I guess that made me sick. I guess he got mad about that. Come to those potlatches just to have his kids get sick.

We stayed with Grandma Bogie at that time. She was awful stingy. We just get little piece of hotcake and few drops of molasses syrup on there. And we don't like that. We were poor people, but we were clean and had lots to eat. Had all kinds of meat and vegetables. Papa always made garden. As far back as I can remember he always raised cabbage, potatoes and turnips. Nothing fancy, but staple food. We always had a lot to eat. My, she was stingy!

Papa talked back to her. I guess that's why he left. She said something about those kids are just spoiled. They wouldn't eat nothing. What's the matter with them. And she baked some dried salmon. Dry dog salmon that they soak in the water overnight. The next morning they bake it in the oven for breakfast. And we wouldn't eat it. We eat staple food. We eat meat and fish and everything, but we never eat old rotten fish. It's good. I know it's nourishment.

And they ate the hotcake with it. We couldn't understand that. Papa said, "Oh, yes, they like to have their hotcake swimming in syrup." That was talking back to his aunt, you know. She didn't like that. I guess that's why he left.

He took me home. A couple of days later he went back down. I stayed with this old lady, his aunt. I didn't mind but, my, I look out the window. Stay at the window. Look down the river on the trail till it's just dark and I couldn't see no more. Waiting for them.

Lewis Landing

A couple of years before Ruby was struck a man, Dave Lewis, built a store up above our homestead. There was an Indian village just across from the mouth of the Yuki, little bit below. That village was called *Noosa Ghunh*. Half mile to three quarter miles above there was Lewis Landing.

At first the village was another place. *Noosa Ghunh* is the Indian name that means right abreast of that big island. That's the island where Papa used to have homestead right on the end, the point is where the houses were. When they

"My great aunt Grandma Bogie with parka, summer rabbit skin inside, the kind that don't shed and fox trim. Buster and I with her in Galena, 1941."

moved the village they took the name with it, even there was no island.

There were a few families living at the village three quarter miles below Lewis Landing. *Saahaaloh* and his family, his brother *Silgee* and his family. William Olin or Olin William and his family. *Olin na* they always call him. Jan Marie and his family. They moved up from Nulato. And there were two, three White people there in a little cabin. And their grandmother and mothers were living there. But we lived up by the store so we never lived in the village.

That's where Papa built a cabin. First he helped Dave Lewis build his store while we lived in a tent. After they finished the store and roadhouse, Papa built our cabin behind there on the side hill. When Ruby was struck we used to sit at the window all day watching these people. Horses, dog teams and guys with a pack on their back necking the sled, Yukon sled. The trail from Flat and Iditarod came out right there. We watch all those people coming to the roadhouse. Some with a few dogs, but they always have to put on a harness and neck the sled with the dogs.

Papa was gone sometime for long time. When he goes to his traps, it's him and my oldest brother. We didn't have no baby. I was the only baby there for long, long time. Towards spring we started to see all these people coming across the river. Necking sleds and with horses. By then Dave Lewis' sister had come in and was cooking for the roadhouse. Mamma used to say don't go down there because she's too busy. So one day we were out sliding down the hill and we see these two women come in. Fancy women. They ride in a buggy, a sled, pulled by horses. A man took them out of the sled and hold their hand and lead them to the door of the roadhouse. We run home. "Mamma! We thought it was old woman but she's young, but I think she's sick. This man is leading her!"

Oh, she gets after us. My! We were a nuisance. They had this big black hat with a big feathers on there. Great big long curly feathers. And their

Little Steamer Gertrude *carried stampeders from Iditarod to Ruby during the 1911 gold rush. Notice the birchbark canoe on the shore.*

Miners traveling with dogs in the Ruby Mining District, 1912.

Keys and Mayhan's leaving for the creeks. Ruby 1912.

shoes was high. They come out of the raccoon blanket, robe, and we thought maybe they were sick people.

That evening we went down again. They used to send things up to Mom to mend like boots and parka, or mitts. So she told us to bring something back down to Dave Lewis' sister. We run down there. Those ladies never stayed in the upstairs. They stayed over at the bunkhouse. So this lady, Lewis' sister, told us to bring these hot water bottle or something. I don't know what it was. We brought it over to this bunkhouse. And these ladies have a curtain down the middle of the room. Make two rooms. We didn't know which one to bring this thing so we just left it right there by the door and started to run out. Somebody called us.

We went back in there and this woman give us some money and hard candy. Fancy womens! Had a robe, silk robes on, and we run out. Rose said, "Let's go back in there." I said, "No, we have to go tell Mom." I tell on her all the time. She's two years older than me, but I tell on her all the time. We ran home. We forgot to bring up the bags down at the store we were supposed to bring home. We brought the candy home and told Mom. She said, *Hutlanee*, don't go there." We asked, "Is those womens sick? What's wrong with them?" We didn't know. She never explained it to us. Long afterwards we found out they were canteen women, prostitutes on their way over to the new gold boom town of Ruby.

Unidentified women in Ruby, 1912.

Photo by Clemons. Alaska Historical Library

Nughutla Gheelinh Dinh

All those people were coming to Ruby but they didn't call it Ruby yet. They had an Indian name for it, *Nughutla Gheelinh Dinh*. It means, "Where the water runs through the slough." Down here at the slough, Ruby Slough, it was the main fish camp. And cross there where Harold Esmailka's fish camp is. All that point up a little ways was an Indian village. That's long, long time ago. And they call it *Nughutla Gheelinh Dinh*. That's where our ancestors came from. They really had a big village there but nobody at the time I remember. Only the graves was visible at the time. Summer of 1911 we moved up there temporarily to fish. I remember because spring of that year my brother Claude was born.

We were at spring camp across from Lewis' Landing. Papa wanted Mamma to go down to the hospital in Nulato to have the baby. See if it will help her save it. He didn't want to give this one away. They give lots away I guess and they didn't live and they lost some. Mamma lost lot of babies. I don't know why. She was a clean woman, but she was always sick when she was carrying. Maybe she didn't eat what she was supposed to. You know they have a way of feeding pregnant womens those days.

They have to eat certain kinds of things to make the bones in the baby. Nowadays they have pills for that. They used to give them more boiled bones in soup for calcium. They eat those and the fish that they bake in the oven and just toast. Papa used to make some out of salmon heads that they smoked and dried. And they toast that just like toast. Like a cracker. That's the salmon heads, bone and all. Mamma used to eat those for the calcium. They eat a lot of things for the babies. They eat some kind of berries that was put up with boiled salmon that was crushed together. That's put away in Indian cold storage underground. Mamma used to eat those for iron.

Anybody could eat it, but the woman who is pregnant with baby can eat more of it. And if there isn't hardly any, well, they save that for the pregnant women. Certain berries they eat and something that they put up in the summertime. I don't quite remember what that is. It's either bark or something. They put it up with berries. It's bitter. Real bitter. They eat it with oil, fish oil, or fat. Moose fat rendered. Tallow. And Mamma wouldn't eat nothing that's fat.

"That's our family except for Mr. and Mrs. Jan Marie and Tom Marie with the mandolin." l-r: 1. Rose Burke 2. Altona 3. Jan Marie 4. Thomas 5. Tom Marie 6. Claude 7. Emily, Altona's mother 8. Big Joe 9. Rocker 10. Mrs. Jan Marie

She was a funny woman. Lot of different foods she wouldn't eat. Papa used to gather up all the duck eggs and things like that in the spring for her. Bring it home. He took good care of her.

So that spring two boys were taking Mamma to Nulato. My oldest brother Thomas and Tom Marie, Jan Marie's son. They picked up her mom in Louden, but as far as they went was Galena. Warm weather, the trail was too soft and too much water. Galena really wasn't a town yet then. Nothing, just a mail relief tent there. And one family, Haemon Henry's folks. They were there for years. That was their home. Easy going people. They don't rush around to get things. The baby was born in that mail tent. After the baby was born they brought her back. Early breakup that year. Water all along the shore. Papa had to go out to the main ice in the river with a boat to bring her into our camp.

Old Man Stickman and my father were good friends. One time he came up to our camp and my Papa gave him a gold watch and gold chain with nuggets on it. I don't know for what. And they used to fill up his boat with stuff. They even gave him my brother. And that one died. We always remember that.

He was year and a half old. He already start talking. He was half-breed. "Okay, I accept it. That's all you need," Papa said to Mamma. She had three of them. They were all brothers. They were all from the same man. Papa said, "When I start to kicking, that's where you want to start jumping around and get scared. But as long as I keep quiet, those are your kids. Those are ours. Leave them alone." He said, "Don't give that baby away." But no, she believed in these medicine people too much. She used to be bad on that.

Of course, her dad was medicine man and her uncles, all her uncles. Her mother and her aunt. Papa's family was same way, medicine people on both sides. They were big people. The kind of people you don't say anything to, but he just break away from them. He never talked. He never talked. So that was the last time we remember they gave Old Man Stickman anything. When they gave him my brother. They come after him in March and in August he fell in a bucket of water, boiling water. Dog feed I think they said. He died right away.

1911

That year the steamboat brought up the people. My brother was born and we moved up here across from Ruby for the summer. 1911. Down on the beach was nothing but tents. The whole hill was nothing but tent. All the way through there down to the bluff of the other end was raft with houses on it. Stores and saloons and a barber shop. Everything was on a raft.

Papa made a camp straight across and Mamma put in a fish net. She was catching fish and selling it. People were coming over right and left to get some fish. She cut some and cleaned them. She was busy. My, she was busy! Papa was up the Melozi cutting house logs for the miners and saw logs. Even sawmill was on raft and they were making lumbers. Then we moved across below the bluff. Papa built a fishwheel and the whole bunch, mother and brother and sisters and grandmother moved in on him.

Indians couldn't mix with Whites those days. They have to have some friend that goes and get the drinks for them. Indians could go in a store, but not in a pool room or saloon or in a restaurant. So Papa run the camp down below the bluff. He made a great big smokehouse out of willow. They all help him. They have to if they want to dry their fish.

They weave willows and make a birch bark roof for the smokehouse. Lot of work, but seems like he's not talking to nobody. He's just going to do what he thinks he's going to do. He never says nothing. Quiet man. He never talked much.

Eight Mile

That winter of 1911 a big sternwheeler *Minneapolis* froze in at the mouth of the Yuki. They got Papa to look after it and in the spring they moved us and all our belongings up to Eight Mile on the boat. Eight Mile used to be Melozi Telegraph Station for the soldiers that had a wire stretched all down the Yukon to Nome. We lived across there then and for a long time. Now Emmit Peters has his fish camp where the station used to be, across the river from Papa's homestead eight miles below Ruby.

They started building the telegraph before I was born, I guess. When we were at *Noosa Ghunh* the whole bunch, soldiers and them, came down in a boat. That's when Mamma, Papa and my aunts used to tell us

32

"These are the people that steals little girls, don't try to talk to them."
So we stay in the house all the time. We didn't know how to talk English
anyway. My brother Thomas could talk English. He learned at Louden.
My aunt used to get so mad when he answer in English.

We lived at Eight Mile for years. We were one family. My big brother,
Thomas Big Joe, two little brothers, Claude and Walter. Then couple
years later she had two more, Lincoln and Rocker. She gave away Walter
down Nulato and Lincoln at Galena and kept the youngest one, Rocker.
Rocker Big Joe. He lives in Nenana now with a big family. He's married
to a great big woman. They had all boys and just two girls. We were
kind of short on our girls. Only my daughter had six girls. Six girls and
five boys. Claude who lives with me here is the oldest one. That's a lot of kids. And she made clothes for those kids. Everything they were raised in and today she's still sewing.

Papa trapped across country in the winter from there. He'd go thirty, forty miles with dogs. Only in a certain time he used to get meat. Early in the spring when the bear is just coming out of the hole, he used to kill bear. 'Cause that's when they're fat and they're clean. And good meat. Oh, we couldn't wait till he killed meat at that time. Then he brings it home. He cooks some out in the camp. He baked them over the

Photo by Clemons. Alaska Historical Library

Ruby waterfront, 1911 or 1912.

fire. That's when I was really enjoying bear meat. I was eating bear meat those days. We were raised with it. But I haven't eaten that now for 45 years because I got sick with it three times. Papa said, "No more." I couldn't believe it, my favorite kind of food.

The girls, teenage girls, not supposed to eat it, you know. But we did. We ate them. Mamma used to get after Papa. He said, "Ahh, they're hungry."

In the falltime in August he used to kill moose. He cut it up and smoke it a little bit then put it down in the cellar. Indian cellar. Cool. It'd keep for months. Nothing spoil down there. It's a deep hole and big as this room, maybe 8' x 8' or 8' x 10'. On top is just level cause he cribs it. First he digs the hole. Then all the way around with logs and moss. Put the moss behind so that dirt can't shift through there. Hewed logs and lumbers. He used most of it inside, the lumber. 'Cause he was up in the sawmill helping with logs so they give him all kinds of lumber. The people down at Louden used to come up and trade something for them. Sometimes he just give it away. They bother him too much. He was good. Papa was good. He was an honest man.

I always tell my grandson honest people is just like having money in the bank. Anybody can help you. Anybody can trust you. That's it. There's no other way around. That's how the Indians were. They didn't have no bank or anything. They didn't have no savings account or nothing. But helping people, that's the way my folks were. They were good people, help people. They never talk about it. They never go bugging people.

Medicine People

Medicine people used to bug people. That's how they got all they want. They don't work. They're worse than the Fathers. Some of the Fathers

back
they
funn
told
M
long
was
and
to go
they
the e
Some
She f
Pe
was a
up ai
She's
tent
of pa
Soi
"You
fer. V
They'
"The
scarec
those
The
We ju
never

were good. Real good. They help people and doctor people but there's only a few like that. Only a few that worked that I know of all my life. And I'm an old people. Father Rossi and Father Jette′ were good people. They could speak Indian and they would come and visit us. They enjoy themselves. Father Jette′ even used to go across to Ruby Slough with Papa. Walking on snowshoes. Oh, they had a big time.

If there was more than one medicine man or woman in a village or if one of the Fathers were there, they would get into arguments and try to take each other's power away. Sometimes they'd all work together too. One time at Louden in the wintertime I went to a meeting of a whole bunch of them. We were staying at Grandma Ann's house way up on the side hill. Her house was just clean. You could eat off the floor she was so clean. I must have been small because I was sitting on the bed, nothing on just some knit socks. My aunt packed me down to the village. Downtown. We have to go up little ways in the back street where this big house was where they were holding this meeting.

We thought it was a meeting but we don't know what they call it because we didn't know how they live in the religion. Mom always scare us to death about these medicine people. We were always scared of them. Lot of people in there. In the middle, close to the doorway was four or five medicine people. Womens with them. And over there was this sick man. I guess they were making medicine. Mamma threw me on the bed. They were all sitting there around the man.

I got scared when they started singing. They were all singing out there. Each one had a blanket over them and talking to somebody. There was nobody. I don't know who they're talking to.

I got scared and started screaming so my aunt covered me up. I guess I went to sleep. Either that or I passed out. I always manage to pass out so I never seen it. I would like to, but I never got to see it.

Another time when I got big, there was one old man that was checking

School

I never went to school. None of us in my family did. We could have gone to school here but at that time you would have to write your life away to get in. Sign a whole lot of papers. Because we're Indian. They didn't let the Natives go to school with the Whites in those days. Anyway, we were living at Eight Mile. If we wanted to go to school, we would have to go down to Louden or Nulato or Koyukuk or maybe up to Kokrines. But we didn't like Kokrines.

Those days Whites and Natives were separate in a lot of things. Goodness, you can hardly walk the street. We did. We went to the show and everything. And when we got bigger we went to the dance in Eagle Hall, big hall up the street in Ruby with Mamma's friends, White womens. Course we didn't dance. We didn't know how. We didn't know what it's all about. Used to be a Native dance hall here someplace too, but I don't know where it was.

And you're not supposed to go in the pool room or the bar. They don't let Indians buy liquor. Nothing. Natives have to have some friend that pick up things for them. But they go to the store alright. I guess their money was the same. Long as you had money they accept it.

The teacher down in Louden, Miss McCormick, got interested in my brother Thomas so he used to go down there. She let him have books. She was real good with him. When he brought home this one big book I guess we were the quietest kids in that house for a long time. Looking at animals.

When I got sick with polio and was in bed, my brother started to work with me. Taught me alphabet. Oh, he had more fun with me than a barrel of monkeys. I read and I just come out with some crazy words.

Rose was going to go to school down Louden. She went down in boat with my uncle Jack Carey. It was falltime and everybody was sick with bad cold, even the teacher. When Rose got there the teacher had already left. Tom DeVane was one of the operators at Melozi Station. He said he could get us in the school. But no, Papa said to leave them at home. "They're learning their own way of living," he said. "That's enough. Later on when they get smart enough, okay. Now they're too crazy. They couldn't learn nothing."

Papa was a teenager when the Bishop got killed at Bishop Mountain. Bishop Seghers. He talked about it lot of times. You know, when we were present. He used

Photo by Clemons. Alaska Historical Library

First Masonic Ball at the Arcadian Hall in Ruby 1911.

to always talk about things that happened. Things that shouldn't happen. He would talk about that in front of us for us to listen, I guess. This is the education in the Indian way. To talk about those things. Like people, when people have a hard time, starving to death and all that. And what they do. And the people that steals. In the end they have a hard time and it all play back on them. And all those things.

Then he take for example. He named the people that was stricken in a

There was a woman in Tanana, Walter Nicholai's wife did that too. Nursed adopted child when she didn't have no children. Then she had to go to the hospital because it caked up and wouldn't give. So they had to do something for her. But Grandmother didn't have help. Maybe that's how she got cancer of the breast.

It was August, starting to get dark when Grandma finally died. She just went to sleep. I don't know if she suffered or not. We were always sitting in the tent with her and she'd talk about lot of things. Whole bunch of women came down from Koyukuk to visit her camp. It was close to Koyukuk. All of them talking all the time and all of a sudden, here they were fixing her up. I don't know when she died. Must have been in her sleep. I was just a kid and didn't pay too much attention to it.

The name of the place was *Kk'uykk'az Dinh*, it meant something like alder, willow place. This was the same place Grandma's real aunt was killed by fish rack. Long time ago they used two tripods with pole on top going to the bank. Then poles across. She was cutting fish in front of that rack. She had pile of fresh willows on the ground and cutting on there. All of a sudden rack full of fish in August fell on top of her and killed her. She was underneath that with her arms spread out. Fish head in one hand and *tɬabaas* in the other.

She was old. I don't know her real name. Everybody call her *Kk'uykk'az Da Tsook'aala.*

"Ann, the beautiful woman who raised my mother. I could never get Mom to tell me what her father's name was. Filka maybe. I don't know. He was Russian."

42

That means old-woman-at-the-place. She was big medicine woman and we're not supposed to use her real name to talk about her, that's the way they used to put it. She did have a name, I guess, but I never know it because they never told us. Not supposed to mention it.

Men was same way, they called them by the children. Like if they have daughter they say, well, that woman's father or that boy's father. Or if they don't have children they always say belong to that place where they been all their life. There's this one crippled old man about the same age as this great aunt, he used to be big medicine man in Tanana. They called him, on-the-other-end-of-the-village, *Donee Kkun' Ghoyit*. That's the only name I know. They never called him by name. The older people maybe know their name, but the younger generation don't. Madeline might know the name because she was well educated by Old Toby. There's a great man there, one of my Pop's cousins. He was real old when he died.

Koyukuk spring gathering circa 1941. l-r: Sophie Sam, her daughter Minnie Yaska, Sally Pilot, Dave Corning, Elizabeth and Henry Haemon, George Attla, Liza Attla, Louie Cleaver, Madeline Solomon, Herbert Solomon.

43

Chapter Two: Fantastic Story

First White People

My Papa grew up mostly around Kateel or mouth of the Dolbi. He was a young man when the first steamboat came up the Koyukuk River. White people and Natives couldn't talk to each other and everybody got scared those days. Before the steamboat, miners used to come from Chandalar to Wiseman and on down the Koyukuk River in Yukon boats. Prospect all the way. Each time they come to a camp all the people run away. They holler and holler for them. But no, they got to run and hide. People got frightened. Once they come out and killed some White people. They were scared. They don't know. And they couldn't understand each other.

So this one old lady, Papa's mother's aunt, *Notok'aghaatIno* had a dream. She was an old lady, big medicine woman. Never had no children. I guess she was married alright. She said she had a dream that there was going to be some boat coming up the river. Great big boat and it works with ashes, coals. Like a great big stove. Well, they don't know what stove is, but it's great big thing and look like rock but it isn't rock and lot of coals in there. And this boat travel by it, she told them. Year before! How did she know?

So a few months later, people had a fish trap in the Ruby Slough. After taking care of their fish, they had nothing to do. They were up on top of the hill just walking, *Kaaltsaa'a* ,the bluff where Ruby graveyard is now. They saw big smoke come up from downriver. They run down the hill to camp at *Nʉghutʲa Gheelinh Dinh*, that's at Ruby. Great big smoke! They don't know what it is. Right on the Yukon. So they watch it. They run up the hill and back down again and everybody is getting all excited.

Pretty soon some womens started packing up. This old girl never said nothing. She was tall, big woman, nice looking. She never said nothing to them. She already told them a year ago what's going to happen. And something tells her no dangers. She went down to the beach and stood there. Came back and said, "No dangers. You guys are foolish."

They all started packing up everything to go up the hill. Then the boat was coming out down at the point. There it comes! And fire is coming out of the thing! She told them, "Okay, this is it. This is happening. This is real. You people don't want to believe me. Go ahead and go. But I wouldn't."

"Oh," they told her, "come on!" Because she's the big one, you know. They rely on her. She's the big medicine woman. And she tell the truth. She tells them what to do and it always happen. She take care of the sick people and she's the only miracle one there that they depend on. They didn't want her to have to get killed.

"Nobody's going to get killed," she said. So she stayed there and all the rest run up the hill. They were gone up there for a long time. Pretty soon two boys come down. She told them, "Stay here with me. Nothing is going to happen. Those are the boat that's supposed to bring supplies up the river." Nobody never told her. No telegraph, nothing. And she told them everything. No, they still wouldn't believe her. They went back up the hill.

The boat was coming nearer. Then it's right next to the village. Real home village was on that side and camp on this side. Nobody in the village, just in camp. Anyway, they see the village is there and they bring out the big horn. They start talking in that in Indian. "Okay," they said, "this is a steamboat. This is a boat that brings supplies village to village from here on out. Don't get scared. This boat got everything in it. And we're the two people that was hired to interpret for them.''

From way over at the point she heard them. So she hollered up to those people, "Come on down. There's Indian talking in that boat. That's a boat!'' They don't know what in the world it is. No, they wouldn't come down.

She went back up to the smokehouse and fixed the fire under the fish, then she went into her little *kk'eeyh yee kkuno*, summer house covered with birchbark, on top of the ground. Winter kind is *naahʉlookkuno*, it's half underground. But this summer one, *kk'eeyh yee kkuno* is made with birchbark and willows so mosquitos don't come in there at all.

Well, she put out all her fancy clothes, like fancy parka and fancy boots. All her goodies she brought out and put them on. Combed her hair and got all fixed up. Put on her summer parka. They used to have a special skin for the summertime. After the animal sheds their winter fur they have this fine fur next to the hide. That's the kind they use in the summertime. Like caribou and deers and things. And small animal. Not moose. For moose they use calf or unborn calf. Either they put it fur in or fur out. Not much fur on them anyway.

The boat was coming closer so she went down to the beach and she beat on her drum. She told the people in the boat, "Everybody got so frightened that they run away. This is fish camp.'' She told them to go ahead and land if they wanted to.

That boat blew its whistle and landed. I guess those poor people was just scared to death up on the hill. She told them to come on in. She wasn't scared. She know what it was. They had hired these two Indians from Nulato to talk for them. They landed and talk to her. Then they took their horn and talk to the people up on the hill. No, they wouldn't come out. So they want her to come on the boat.

They asked her a few questions like how they lived and what they got and what they do. What they want to sell or trade. I don't know what she had. Something to trade. Anyway, they give her brown sugar cubes. And they gave her some beads. Fancy trade beads for some fur she had. Some kind of tanned skin she had. Pretty soon they gave her a drink of some kind. She drink that and soon she was all drunked up. They gave her a red bandana and they put that on her head. Just really having a lot of fun with her. She wasn't afraid. She knew about sugar and tobacco because her folks used to go to Selawik cross country from Koyukuk and they used to have this stuff. Like tobacco and sugar and salt. She knew about those.

She traded some dry fish and wooden spoons. Whatever she has. They say she was pretty good woman. She make everything. She even make birchbark canoes by herself. By now she was getting to feel pretty rough. She thought, "Goodness, what's happening to me?" So she asked these Native people and they told her it's vodka, Russian stuff. Then she told these mens to take her ashore. No, they didn't want her to go. They want to keep her there and get her drunk. She said, "No, get me off the boat. If you don't get me off the boat I'll tell you what you're going to do. You're going to sink going upriver."

So they took her off the boat. The captain gave her a dog. Big red dog with long ears and little white spot here and there. "*Ahnaa*," she says. She don't want it. What's she going to do with it? They say feed it anything. So they give it to her and groceries and beads, calico, everything she dreamt about was on that boat.

Finally a couple people came down the hill. She was feeling pretty high. She told them to tell their Papa to come down and trade. Get some tobacco. She want them to trade some tanned skins for it. So they all come down and met these two interpreters from Nulato and traded. But they wouldn't give anyone else a drink. Just that old girl. Her name was *Notok'aghaatIno*.

Starvation

1900 was a hard year. A lot of people died, mostly babies. Starved to death. No snow and a hard time to get anything that's alive. They used to dig into beaver houses and spear them. They had no traps or steel snares. But that winter everything was froze up. No snow and cold. People went cross country from Louden about sixty miles to Sulatna, where we call Tamarack now. The original Indian name for that creek is *Tsolaatno*, White people cut it short and call it Sulatna. "No" means river. They always have a reason to name a place. What it's like or what happened. That's always a good country for caribou in the winter. 1900 just a very few people made it. Big camp, people from Kokrines and Louden meeting in Sulatna. They lost a lot of kids. Starved before they got there. Mom and Papa were already married and went there with their folks.

They ate up all their romaine off the sleds and off the snowshoes. They cook those to eat. And few people catch couple squirrels. No rabbits. They must have had a tough time. They try everything, but no snow. And some of the women let their baby go and nursed their husbands. To keep them alive. Let their baby die. Starve. Oh, it must have been awfully sad.

They couldn't catch beaver. They try everything. They tried muskrats in the lakes. And no blackfish. Blackfish was the main food for those people that's unable to do anything for themselves because they're easy to catch. They live in the lake in the moss and water. Hardly any water. That's what people lived on lot of times. But there's none on this side of the cross country where they went. And they don't have the kind of equipment to make great big work through the ice and all that to catch fish. They were getting weaker.

One day my grandfather's sister lost her daughter. She went over to her brother and was going to club him to death. She took half burned wood out of the fire. They had fires inside their spruce bough teepees that they used for shelter. She went over to my grandfather's place and was going to kill him because her daughter died. She said, "It's on account of you. You're the medicine man. You're supposed to save these people." Raised Cain with him.

He never said nothing. They say the man never talked much. He felt bad. Finally he told her, "We feel bad enough, this happening. Don't make it any worse."

That day he took a long walk someplace. What he could do, you know. Little what he could do. He was starving himself. On his way back he picked up acorn. Spruce cones. One of those big bunch. You've seen them. They're almost green, reddish. Young and they look like grapes. He brought that home. He put it in a bucket in the fire. Started boiling it. He was making miracles. He didn't tell nobody what he was doing.

They were camped under this hill. What they call Tamarack now. There was caribou on there but they couldn't get near it. Soon as they think it's down at the bottom of the hill and they surrounded it, whoever could move around a little bit, they run out. Couldn't get one even.

Grandpa was thinking, wishing, I guess, all the walks he made. Down the creeks and up a little ways. As far as he could walk. Mom always talked about that, about how he suffered for his people. Just because he was a medicine man and everybody figured why don't he make a miracle and something good would happen. Well, long time ago that's what they used to do 'cause they lived off the country. They didn't have White man grub, just sugar and tea. Very few things they had. So he picked up those spruce cones and when he got home he put it to boil.

Five other men were out that day. Gone all day. This one old lady that's well-to-do chopped little piece of fish with some fat to go with it. Put it in a bag for each one of them. Little bit. Very little to live on.

Grandpa called the people over for a meeting. And these ladies gave up the last they had for the people in the meeting. They all had a little to eat. He told them, "This is the last we have. Tomorrow we don't eat unless you people help me make a wish. You people know how to do it. I can't do it alone. I got to have assistance. I'm not strong anymore." His sister came over and told him she was sorry that she was going to beat him up. She didn't mean to. She got crazy like 'cause she was hungry and lost her daughter. It was a big girl.

Then those five guys came home and brought a little fawn. Little caribou. I don't know where it came from but it was on the glacier when they were coming home. Grandpa told them to put it on something clean and cut it up. Butcher it up and everybody eat.

I always think about it. Fantastic story. Especially when I used to go out and hunt. How did they do it? My background. Can that happen to me?

So they cook this fawn and that feed the whole village. Whole camp. And then grandpa told them to build a big house, make it good and sturdy so it wouldn't fall. And the one's able go get some wood, put it all one place. Stand it up so it don't get under the snow. His place was big too so they all move in these two places. And he told them take snowshoes, whoever still had snowshoes they didn't eat, and sleds. Stick them up around the house near the door. He said, "This is what we're going to do. We're not going to move no more. We have no more strength. Nobody don't have no more strength. Okay, just don't move. Once you get in here and make yourself warm don't move. This is final. I can't do no more for you guys. This is it, it's me, I'm going to go first."

They all did what he said and he give them cup full of this broth, boiled spruce cone. On the top, must have been the pitch, was glazed just like fat. And the broth they said was just like when you throw fresh blood in hot boiling water and it curdles. He gave everybody, all the one he think that's going to work, a cup of this broth. He put the rest in the fire, cones, what's left in the bucket.

Each family saved a little piece of meat and they folded up the skin. They'll eat this later. Then everybody went to sleep. Just like taking pills. They were so weak. They drank this broth then eat those meat. Just knock them out. They must have slept for about two days. Papa said one time he woke up and wanted to go to the bathroom, relieve himself, but he went right back to sleep. Didn't go. They were so weak.

Pretty soon somebody said, "Hey!" and another one, "*Oho!*" Papa started listening. Grandpa said, "*Snaa*, something is happening."

Snow and blowing. All the time they were sleeping. Somebody hollered, "Over there!" In Indian, you know, "*Donggu, donggu doonoogha*" (meaning "something is there" E.J.). They're telling one another. People look out the door. The place was just covered. All blown over. Like nothing there. How long they slept they don't know. Papa said he know one time he wanted to go to the bathroom so bad. And turn over and went back to sleep. That was it. He never know nothing after that. Just sleep.

Somebody holler, "Over there!" Another one, "Yeah." And, "Tell them." They all start talking to one another between the houses. Papa look out. His brother-in-law was just getting up. He was in a good mood. He teased Papa, "Your clothes will freeze to you. You have been wetting yourself a long time." Papa open up the flap and the place was just covered. Blowed over. And over toward the bottom of the hill they could see a little clearing. It was just horns after horns and they all move. It was caribou heads. He said he just fall back. He was going to say something but he just fall backwards. Grandpa said, "*Snaa*, my son..." Papa told him, "Yeah, they're over there."

Grandpa drag himself up. This guy wetting himself already put his heavy clothes on. Grandpa made it to the doorway and looked out. "*Oho*," he said, "*Oho*." Then he praises it. "*Baasee',* dear God, *bassee'.*" Whatever he was talking to he was praising it.

He woke the womens up. They all put their heavy clothes on. Snow up to their waist. They could hardly walk. Just three big dogs they saved. They feed them camp robbers and even the mice. Maybe dogs eat each other, I don't know. Whatever they could get they fed them to keep them alive. Just barely alive and that's it.

When they get outside they send message to one another. Talk to one another. If they got their gun ready. Someone said, "Yes, okay, let's try it." Those caribou couldn't move the snow was so deep.

Those womens got all excited. They crawled. They didn't have no snowshoes. They already cooked them up a long time ago. So they crawled. Men went off on each side. Told them to go in the middle. And they made a killing right there. They clean up the whole thing.

Caribou try to run but can't. So much snow. Deep. It's soft, not settled yet. Just like soup. Papa said that's the first time he ever see his mom go over to his papa and love him up. She thank him for that, before anything should happen to her babies.

Everybody eat. They don't do nothing but eat. And they repair all their snowshoes, sleds and everything. They camp right there all spring. Come out with canoe after breakup. That was in May they came out. That September is when the diptheria epidemic struck and lot of people died. Grandpa was one. 1900.

Chapter Three: Polio

Polio

(This chapter is drawn almost exclusively from tapes Gladys Dart recorded during her year teaching in Ruby).

I must have been 7 years old because that next year we went down to visit Grandma before she died in Louden. We were playing on the beach. Hopscotch. Rose and I. My brother, Tommy, and his friends were up the beach hunting grouse. It was in the evening. After supper. Must have been in August because it started to get a little dark at night. Nice beach there at Eight Mile. It goes way out. We already got tired of looking for agates, must be a million of them down there, and we were hopscotching.

All of a sudden I fell down. I tried to get up but I couldn't. I started rolling around. Rose was laughing. Oh, she just laugh, laugh, laugh, laugh. I told her to come on help me up. And I start crying. But she just kept laughing because I looked so funny she said. Then I scream at her. I always did anyway. Like some other kids we were always fighting.

I guess my brother heard me from way up the beach. She was always beating me up. Even threw me overboard. She used to be rough with me 'cause I cry too much. I cry about everything. Well, I couldn't help it because I was the baby for a long, long time. We didn't have no tiny baby. I was the youngest. Finally my brother came down.

best you can do. They don't do that at the hospital. They just let you lay there and give medicine.

Papa got king salmon head, dried one. He baked it in the oven until all the drip came out. Greasy king salmon head. When he put it in the oven it stunk. That's the grease they used to rub me down so my skin won't get irritated. And I don't know if it was bear grease or goose grease they used too. Pretty soon they run out of those things and used some other oil.

The soldiers came over from Melozi Station whenever they could. Examine me. Talk about me. They could send me down to Seattle, but it would take long time to go on the boat down there. Then they talk about hot springs. But Mamma was against hot springs. She used to be afraid of them. I don't know why. She has reasons I guess. She said you have to know about it. You have to understand the thing. What you're not to do or what you have to do with these hot springs. She used to be awful careful about a lot of things. Papa agreed with her.

He told me when they were going to the Forty Mile country they came to a hot spring. The others took a bath but he wouldn't. He just wouldn't. You have to know about it he said. He had some rocks or something in his pocket that he found on his way. Pretty rocks he said. He put that in the water and then dipped the water out of there to drink. His folks used to put bones of animals like bear in the water. Or tooth of bear or wolverine or something that's tough animal. They use that to exchange with the water. Just like buying it.

Around January or February it start to subside. Then I can sleep. They keep on massaging me. Then in March my brother made crutches for me. One leg is out fine, the other one is still all curled up. He said, "You don't rely on these. You use it but you use your feet."

Oh, he was rough with me. It was just hurting me. He put up some poles and I have to swing on those things. I was good on that. And my grip, my hands were good. He would hang me up there by my legs and I try to catch the other pole. Swing. Ahh! Then I scream and scream. When it warmed up he put some outdoors. And he made slides. We played on that. That's how he cured me. And shock.

I'd be hobbling on the crutches and he'd come right behind me and kick the crutches from under my feet. I'd fall right in a puddle face down. That's to shock me. And he throw me in the creek two or three times.

Father Rossi or Father Jette came up from Louden and said electric shock would be good too if he could get it. He let him have a battery. Old fashioned box battery with two things you grab hold of. But it almost killed me. I passed out. Papa said, "No. Don't do that to her. I think that sickness weakened her heart. We don't want it."

March, then I could hobble over to the door on crutches. My brother would open the window and he built a certain bench that I could sit on. In front was a big tree. He trimmed that off and made a trap for a squirrel. And I was catching it. Anything to attract my mind so I don't hurt. Anything at all.

He taught me how to use bow and arrow too. Kids weren't allowed to monkey with guns. Not girls. We used that bow and arrow to hunt willow grouse, ptarmigans, rabbits, anything. I killed a squirrel once. It ran up the tree with my arrow. Its guts was hanging out and everything. I never used it after that. I just wouldn't. When I see that animal running around dragging its stomach around. I didn't like it. Made me sick. Gee, that squirrel was tough to kill.

I started to cry so Papa shot it down with a .22. He thought I was crying for my arrow. But he found out later I wasn't. I cried for that squirrel. I don't know what made me want to kill it. I used to play with those all the time. I didn't think I was going to hit it because it was jumping tree to tree. Here I shot. And I caught him in the stomach.

bothering me and I hollered for Mom. They got words over that. So he didn't never bother me for a long time. Papa said, "You should tell him to go back up to Kokrines where they live like dogs." He say, "That girl is too young." And I was his baby. I was Papa's special one. That's how I got my name.

Altona is half of a long Indian word — *Sakkonh gheeltonee*. It means, "It laid inside of me." He had a way of saying it. That's the way it's supposed to be. When he came out of Novi and came down to my great aunt's place where I was born and first saw me, that's what he said. And it stuck to me ever since. Marie was the name I was baptized with.

Anyway, I raised Cain with that man, John Slaveenga, for a long time. Then he took me up to below Tanana where his uncle the medicine man lived. I got pregnant and I had my baby when I was 13. December 22, 1918. We weren't married. We were blessed by Father Jetté in Tanana, but he couldn't marry us. I don't think John could get a license. I was too young. Father Jetté told him to send me home. "What do you mean picking up children. What's the matter with Big Joe's family? I know those kids. She's just a baby." We knew him from Kokrines. He used to be stationed there

Arrival of Tanana guests in boats at the Kokrines potlatch June 28, 1918. Photo by Jette.

Kokrines potlatch, woman dancing. June 28, 1918. Photo by Jette.

62

running the little Catholic mission. He gave John a written note to take to Big Joe. "Take her home," he said. "When she's old enough, go back and pick her up."

He didn't take me home. He's that kind of people. He laugh. He think that was a big joke. He said, "I can't take her home 'cause she's going to have baby." Everytime I think about it I wonder how can my folks let him take me like that.

John didn't want to wait. He already had two wives that died on him. No wonder. They probably worked to death. He was lazy man. I wouldn't talk to him. We lived together three years. Only when it's necessary I talked. And I worked.

After his wives died, he lived with Henry Titus' mother for a couple years. They didn't have any kids. Then she married Old Man Titus and they had kids. Then I had this boy. It was his kid, yes, but I have to grow up with him. I cried everytime he's hungry. It was just terrible. If it wasn't for my folks I guess the baby would die from hunger. I was too young to know what to do for it. I nursed that baby for about three and a half years. I didn't know any better.

Fall of 1920, my oldest brother Thomas died. Drowned down at Eight Mile. Papa couldn't live there anymore. We moved up here. That's when John started getting rough. The baby was a little over two years old. Gee, John started to get rough.

My sister had her baby after I'd had mine. Then she had to wait for her husband. He was an army man. He went Outside. They took all of them Outside from Tanana that time. Burk had to go too. Old Man Burk. She had to wait for him. Already she had two babies from him before they were married. Then John decided Rosie was the one he should marry. "Oh, I made a mistake. I should have taken Rosie," he said. Like he's really gonna have his pick.

And we were good kids. Understandable. Get along with anybody. You

Rosie and Belena's mother, Aunt Jenny Jacob circa 1929.

"My uncle Ivan Hardluck and John Slaveenga." Kokrines circa 1914.

Rosie Burk circa 1927.

couldn't make him understand that. It got so I didn't try. I never talked to him. Everytime you turn around you're doing something wrong. You're layed up with these men and everytime you look at somebody you're making eyes at them. Jealous! Oh, he was evil. He even accused us of our own brother. I don't know if he was over sexy or what. I couldn't understand. I was just a little kid. Next month, in January, I'd be fourteen when I had my first baby.

Papa caught him pushing me around, trying to choke me with my mitt strings. I had my mitts on and he grabbed them and shut the door on the strings. Pulled on it. Almost choke me. Papa came up around in the back door. Here I was choking. He opened the door and here was John holding the mitts. Still he tried to lie that it wasn't him. Who else could it be? I kind of got mad. Papa told him to get out.

He was just mean and I didn't know what life was all about. He finally found out that I didn't care for him I guess and I was growing up. He was afraid I was going to leave him. We had rented a house up the hill. I sewed all summer and tanned mooseskin to get that house. Sold fish to buy grub. He wouldn't do nothing. Laugh and just happy-go-lucky. Long as he had somebody to work for him he should be happy. But that was it. Papa said just bring her home.

I talked to John Dunne, a lawyer here. I went to him. I was scared. Papa took me back but I was scared. I told him my brother got drowned in September and I was all alone. He was the only one that told me what to do and took care of me. I went to see the lawyer. He asked what I came there for. I said I'm going to stay home now. I'm not going back to this awful man. I told him how old I was. He had been lying about my age all along.

The lawyer said, "What's wrong with that?"

"I'm scared of him," I said. "I have no way of defending myself."

"Just let me handle that, okay," he said. "You go home. It'll cost you $500 for a divorce. Where did you get married?"

"I didn't," I told him. "This Joe Dean, the lawyer in Tanana gave him a piece of paper in Tanana for him to bring me home and leave me home and pick me up when I was old enough to get married. Father Jetté told him the same thing but he wouldn't do it. He lied about those."

"So okay," he said, "I'll talk to your dad. You stay home."

That was it. But I went back to him on account of the baby. He didn't like his dad, but just the same I thought the baby should have his own dad. I was just a kid. I didn't know. I couldn't think. People start talking. Even though, that didn't last long. I moved back to Papa and John went to Kokrines.

My Baby Dies

I kept the baby. Five years old when he died. I already was married again and just had another baby. We didn't even know he was sick. A while after he had measles, Dad, I call my second husband Dad, took him up to Big Creek in a canoe.

He said he didn't act right. Tired and he went to sleep in the canoe. Well, anybody could go to sleep in a canoe. You or me. But my son was always anxious to see ducks or see fish get caught. Then he wasn't interested. Doggone it, a couple weeks after that he died. He had mastoid. That's an earache and some abcess or something. It's supposed to break out. All the kids get it. Most of them go deaf.

We were at camp. One day he got up and the baby cried. He came down to where we were cutting fish and said, "Mom, the baby cried." And he grab hold of his head. Standing there. Dad looked up. "Did he fall? Did you see him fall?"

I went up to him. I didn't pay much attention to the baby. I caught hold of him and said, "What's the matter?" He said, "My head hurts."

Dad came up asked about him. We right away let the fish go and brought him down to Ruby. Took him to the doctor living across the street, Doctor Ross.

Doc Ross examined him and said he had a fever. No way to get him to the hospital. There was a hospital at Tanana but the boat already went by. Steamer is the only way to go unless you go by small boat. How I cried. Because that's after my brother drowned. He used to take care of the whole family. No matter what it is. Wintertime he put on his skis and a packsack and away he go. Go to Galena or anyplace where you can get help. Doc Ross said put him to bed.

Dad went back up to camp to get somebody to finish the fish up. He brought the baby back down. Madeline Notti and the family was across the street. The Pitka family. She wasn't married yet then. She took the baby home to take care of it.

When I came back in he was walking around. I told him he wasn't supposed to be up. He went to the closet and took all his toys out. "What are you doing with that? I asked him.

"I'm going to put them under my bed," he said. "Those are going to be the baby's."

So he put them all under the bed. I never think nothing. Then Mamma come up. She prayed for him and everything. I told her what he did. She never said nothing to me. Mamma know that the kid was awfully sick but she wouldn't tell me. She told me to go get things ready in the kitchen. Cook up something. She went out for a while.

Pretty soon whole bunch of people come in. The boy went back to bed. I said, "You're sleepy?"

"No," he said. "Sit by me."

We had a little cot for him in the bedroom. I sit by him and start talking killed you know. Soft. He said, "Walk on it." Everybody was quiet. I walked on it like he told me to. I was glad to. And he took me and rubbed my face on it's head. Ohhh! Oh my, what a roar came out with that! Papa said something to him and they almost fought. He said, "Why didn't you bring your own children to this kind of a stuff to do that. Why my daughter?" I was always his special one. Nobody never said nothing.

My brother went over there, picked me up and put me on the sled. Papa said, "You take her home. You shouldn't have brought her up over here." He said something else about, "I hope that she has a good work and all that. And live a long time to see things come true, and all those things." He said that because this man, his cousin, had lost two daughters the year before. Papa thinks that's why his cousin doesn't like other people's kids. Papa's so mad he just want to hurt him I guess by saying that.

Go Listen for Something

Papa always come back to me. I was with him one time, down the slough. I must have been about eight or nine years old. I want to go with him. I was just starting to walking good, after having polio. I wobbled a little bit. It was the falltime. The next year. My brother said, "I guess that'll do her good." Mom said, "Naa, the ground is too frozen and she might step into wrong place. Her legs are weak." My brother said, "No, she got to exercise those legs." So I went with Papa.

He was going back there looking for a porcupine. Long time ago, they never used to say the name of the bear, or talk about it in front of womens. That's bad luck. When they're going to go hunting for bear, they'll tell their company, I'm going to go listen for something. Some noise. She understands right away, and says, yes. That means he's going hunting bear. They have a round-about way of telling one another. They don't come out and just say, "I'm going to hunt a bear," or "I seen one."

So I went with him. Into the slough. It was a long ways on that big island, way out there where our cabin was. We walked, walked, walked, walked. I look up at the trees once in a while. There was no porcupines in sight. I don't know where they're at. I couldn't find them. He said, "You're tired?"

"No. I want to go some more. I'm going to see that porcupine up in a tree."

He stopped. And for his lunch he always had chopped up fish. Dried fish, skin and all. Little cubes cut fine. Then he takes the dried and smoked moose fat and put them in there. And a handful of raisin. And meat, dry meat. Shredded with knife. You ever shred those dry meat with knife, and they curl up? Oh, it's good. Just like chipped beef but it's all curled up. Sometimes he put walnuts in there. Put all that in a little old canvas bag in his pack. That's his lunch. Lunch bag from way back. They always put it under their belt and eat it middle of the day. I see these people float downriver in summertime. They have seeds and all kind, put together same way. I always think of Papa. That's the grub they say.

Well, that was Papa's grub. Eat that as soon as they get hungry. And melt some ice, or drink some water if they come to the water. "Never drink overflow," he told me. "Never, unless you cook it. Make tea out of it. And eating snow. Don't do it." You seen overflow? You'd get tired if you drink that. Awful tired and more thirstier than ever. He said, "The best thing to do is take top of those spruce trees, the very end, and chew that. It's bitter, the boughs. Well, that's what you need. Chew that like gum and swallow the juice. Forget about the bough. Spit that out later.

Rocker with his father Big Joe circa 1917.

71

didn't have dogs anymore. Before anybody know that I even got there I get hold of Holt. He was the pilot. I asked him to fly me to Kateel this afternoon. I got all my stuff with me at the airport. Airport was inside of the dike at that time. Just like that. We took off. Nobody know I went over there. Just like I sneaked away. I always just take off. Those days, nobody was scared to take me. Now they wouldn't take me. They're afraid of my heart, my pacemaker. They want to have doctor's orders.

So we went. Albert Dayton and his family were there. Madeline was gone already. Johnson Toby had gone with her. Albert got there after they were gone so I stayed with Albert and his family. That's when Albert Dayton was taking me all over. All excepting the trail going to Selawik where his brother John got killed. He wouldn't take me out there. I said, "Albert, why don't you take me over to Madeline?" He said, "Oh my, that's way over to Horseshoe Mountain, pretty near it."

"Well, that's nothing. You have good dogs," I said.

"No," he said, "I can do better than that. I'll let you trap with me." And I trap all the beaver that he couldn't catch. Gee, clear water. You could see down the bottom where they been. You could even see his track. The beaver. So clear. I caught five beaver. At Andrew Pitka's camp Albert said is just old beaver. Old wise one. Couldn't catch them. We were there when the plane landed.

Here comes Herbert. Back already. There was nothing wrong with him. He start to have that cough every now and then. That's when he should quit drinking and smoking right there. He would have still lived today. That's what the doctor told him. Herbert said, "Where's Madeline?"

I said, "I don't know. She wasn't here when I got here. Albert and his family was here. I'm staying with them." He stayed that night. Next morning Albert look for him and he was gone. He had walked. Followed their trail. I said to Albert, "Is it long ways?"

"Oh ho, long ways. You could never make it." I thought to myself, he don't know that I can walk on snowshoes.

Well, he was gone three days. I was with Albert and them all that time. I said, "You think he'll be alright?"

"Oh yes. He'll be alright."

Herbert walked maybe thirty-five miles to the Horseshoe Mountain. It took him all day and half of that night. Then he dug up that snow and sleep in there. Cover himself up with snow. When he woke up he heard the dogs barking. Here it was just little ways from Madeline's camp, about four miles.

He said to his wife, "What in the world are you doing out here? Your sister is waiting in camp."

She said, "What the heck we're waiting for then?"

They hook up the dogs and turn around, came back and got me. They left Johnson at the camp. It was three days when they come back. After she loved me up, she said, "Well, what are you doing over here at Albert's tiny cabin? There's a great big house and nice big bed." So I went next door to their cabin. That day she baked bread and got everything all ready. We spent two nights there and then get ready to take off back to Horseshoe Mountain. All morning. Dogs barking. They put kids in the sled.

Oh dear. I got tired of waiting. I put on my snowshoes and left. Eleanor, her daughter, went with me. That's all flat country. After we walked up the little hill she lay down on the trail. She got tired. I didn't know I was walking too fast for her. Big woman. She was already married and had a kid. I keep looking back. I thought she'll get up and follow me, but she didn't. So I walk and walk and walk and walk. I look at the time. My goodness, it's three o'clock. I thought I must be pretty close to their camp. But where are they? They had fifteen dogs with a great big sled. He's on the gee-pole and she's on the back as usual.

I broke down a lot of branches. You know I didn't have no ax, no gun, nothing. Going in that strange country. I never even thought. I just leave all those things with the sled. And I never been over there before. So I make a big long place with the broken branches. Then I made a big fire. I pack wood and pack wood and then I lay down. The sun started going down and it cooled off. It was about the middle of March. Because April 4th is when I killed that bear. I feel so mad everytime I think about it. Because I seen it alive. That head right on top of the snow looking at you and I didn't have my camera.

They finally came and we ate lunch there. They had Eleanor on the sled. He said, "Did she say she's not going to come?"

"Oh, I waited for her but I think I walk a little too fast. I don't run or anything. Just steady pace. I always do, when I'm out on snowshoes. When I put my snowshoes on, it's just everything goodbye. I go." Even now, as old as I am, I have to walk on snowshoes. I take off.

We finally went into their camp. Everybody was busy. We was there about a week, I guess. They were all eating beaver meat. I didn't want to eat it. I couldn't never eat it anyway. So I was catching rabbits. I set a few traps for beaver. I can't catch them with snares. I guess I catch them but it takes me long time to get it right. I rather use traps. There's lot of things they're superstitious about trapping beaver. I never was with my own people that tell me those things so everything I do is *hutlanee, hutlanee, hutlanee, hutlanee.*

One morning Madeline refused to go with Herbert and Johnson. As a woman, at certain time of month they don't go. They stay home and out of the way of their mens. That's *hutlanee.* I learn lots of their ways since I was with her. I learn from Rebecca Jimmy, too, when I trapped with her before. Oh, she got after me. I ask her how come

Photo by Altona Brown. Altona Brown Collection

Madeline and Herbert Solomon with children. "That's out Kateel where I made a fire and they catch me up with dog team. From there they said no more walking and put me in sled."

Mamma didn't tell us those things when we were small. Like certain part of a moose or a bear you don't eat. We eat everything we want out of it when we were kids. Even the bear head. Papa cooked it.

I thought Madeline had a lot of guns so didn't bring no gun with me. I went and cleaned this .22 long. The end of it was sawed off about an inch or two. They had some black tape around it for a sight. I don't know whose gun that was. Must have been Johnny's, her first husband. So I took that. She said, "Where you going?"

Madeline and Herbert Solomon, Johnson Toby, Naddie and Jennie at their Kateel camp in 1949.

"I'm going to walk up the hill." We were camping about twenty miles from this big mountain, almost behind Galena. Horseshoe Mountain they call it. *Hulkkaagha yila'* is Indian name for it. I remember that hill very good because I was there when I was a little girl and I lost my mitts. We were camping. I was sitting there swinging my mitts on their string and off it goes in the bonfire. So I want to go back to that hill. I haven't been there long time. Madeline didn't want to go, she says there's lot of brown bear. But it's wintertime so I put on my packsack. I'm going.

There's a knoll down the bottom where we had the camp. I went straight up the hill. I got up there and here Madeline is right behind me. She didn't say she was coming. Eleanor was at home with the two girls. I didn't go very far before I got to these spruce trees. Nice spruce trees with big boughs. I was right on top and here the spruce chicken flew up. I was hungry for something besides rabbit. Spruce chickens sitting up there, right above me. Nothing to keep me from hitting it.

I shot whole box. Gee, I was disappointed. I blamed the gun. Finally Madeline come over. She was over on the bank side looking at holes. I don't know what kind. I guess she was looking for bear holes. She told me they don't believe in that. The woman's not supposed to look for bear holes. That's *hutIanee*. You're not supposed to go near there. She come over and said, "What are you shooting at?" I'm on my last box of shells and they just sit there. Whole bunch of them sit there so cozy. I told her to look where they were. "Just like blueberries," she said.

I told her, "Okay, you shoot them with that high-toned gun." She shoot and shoot. Pretty soon, one at a time they started to fly away. We finished pretty near the box. Nobody hit nothing. I said, "You go back to camp and get another box of shells." I cleaned the gun. I dropped a nail in there and pulled a rag through. Then I loaded up with seven shells. I was mad. Just boiling over. Here was all kind of meat I could eat besides rabbit.

She come back with shells, all sweaty. She said, "What do you want to walk for? We can't kill nothing with this gun." I didn't say too much. We were walking on top of the hill. Here was a rabbit! Good target. I took the gun and shoot, shoot, shoot. Nope. I shot all seven shells. Then Madeline reload and shot about four times. It hopped away. By that time I wanted to take that gun and smash it right against a tree. I was getting upset everytime I put shells in it.

I don't know what keep one of us from killing rabbit. That I didn't feel too bad about. I felt too bad about spruce chickens because I used to knock it's head off, even in the moonlight. I reloaded. She kind of felt bad but didn't say nothing. I walk down the slope. Down the saddle. Then I just get lively and happy. Papa's words hit me. I thought, maybe that's it. Never happened to me before. But maybe Papa's words is going to come true.

I started walking and wishing for a camprobber or something for target. But no, I don't believe in shooting target. Just aiming at nothing. She said, "Where we going? Sister, where we going? Let's go back." I didn't say nothing to her. She didn't have to go with me. I didn't ask her to. And couple times they went out without me. I thought maybe they didn't want me to trap with them. So I was catching these ones that they couldn't catch. I was funny. I was stranger there.

We went over two saddle. Then I walk out toward the big lake they call Coffeepot Lake. The original name was *Beedoy Litonh Dinh*, big lake. Beautiful country. We came down to clearing where there's no trees. I see where somebody had been walking. I told Madeline. She said, "Oh yeah, that's old Andrew Pilot's camp. Some people been over here and try to head us off from this beaver trapping.

I look all around at this trail and thirty to forty foot knoll that's all blowed over. Madeline want to know what I'm looking for. I ask her, "Did you ever see wolverine make beds out of these spruce boughs? Or did somebody tell you?" Because she's more educated than I am in Indian. She had old people that she lived right amongst like Young Toby. She said, "No, I never heard of it. What do you think you'll find down there?"

I give her my snowshoes and said, "Hit that." Well, she didn't know what she was looking for or maybe she refused to know. So I took my snowshoes and shovelled away the snow. I gave her my ax. I always took ax, two snares, piece of rope and knife in my pack. So I gave my small double bitted ax to her. She said, "What am I going to do with it?" I told her to hit around and see if she can find something. So she was hitting and pull out spruce bough. "Oh, oh," I said. Somebody had to make bed there." She keeps saying that's Andrew Pilot's camp and somebody was over here.

I got on top of this knoll. Madeline was about three feet below me. I thought I saw something but I wasn't sure. I turned around and here was a bear head on top of the snow, about twenty feet away. Right on top of the snow, looking this way! Great big ears. And it went back down. I said, "Ahhhhh! I should have taken my camera!"

She jumped up and said, "*Ginee? Soda, ginee*? What's wrong?" But it already went down.

I said, "Get your snowshoes on." "*Ginee*?" she said. "What you see?"

She put her snowshoes on. She had a dress and long parka. She wouldn't wear slacks or jeans in those days. She come up where I was. I say, "Stand there. Now hit that tree." So she was hitting it. I looked down and here he'd stuck his head out again. I know then it's really bear. "Look!" I said.

She grabbed me and said, "Let's go home. We already seen it. Let's go home, we'll tell Herbert and Johnson." I wouldn't even listen to her. We come close to it. Maybe fifteen feet away. In Indian she say, "*Soda, anaa'* don't. Don't go, we'll go home. I know where the trail is. We'll hit the dog trail and go home." But I'd seen it and I'm not going to leave it. Even if I have to kill it with ax. I put my pack back on.

She said, "Remember sister, we couldn't hit nothing with that gun. How you think we're going to get it?" She keep talking, but I didn't say no more. I start walking over there. We was about ten feet away from hole. Snow is deep. I shot below the hole about three feet. I heard him growl. Then he stuck his head out. I just boom, boom, boom. It went down. I looked for her. She's right by me with this ax all ready to go. She was just sweating. I grab her and said, "We got it!"

"I don't know" she said. I went over there. "What are you going to do?" she said.

"I'm going to see if it's dead." So I reload the gun, go over there and took off my snowshoes. Here was the hole. Big enough for his head and shoulder. I stuck my snowshoes down there. I was ready. I know what to do. I thought, I'll just throw my snowshoes and start shooting. I stuck my snowshoes down there and start shaking it. It was just like jelly. I start singing. Teasing her.

We had a tough time to drag it out. And then she had an idea that there was some more in there. She said, "Sometimes there's two or three that live in one den." Maybe she's right. I don't know. I don't know nothing about them. That's the first time I ever went to the bear hole since I was a little girl and I went with Papa.

We tried everything to get it out. I had a rope but when I bend down I get dizzy. I said, "Okay, you try. There's nothing wrong with your heart."

"Okay, you hold me," she said. She got brave. So I was hanging on to her and she reached down there and put that beaver snare around it's neck. We made a tripod with that rope hanging down. Then we use dry pole to pry it out of that hole. All our weight on the end of that pole. Finally we got it up. Great big black bear. Boy, it was fat. Good meat and beautiful skin. I don't know when I took my hunting knife out of my packsack, but all I had was Papa's pocket knife. We used that and butchered it up.

I was the only one had packsack so she just took out the best part of the innards and put that in the packsack and left. I took my inside shirt and hung that up, and my gloves that I used to butcher it up. "Why are you going to leave your parka here?" she said.

"Oh, just for fun. So that wolverine or something wouldn't go near it. Wolf or something." Lots of them there.

When we came home, Johnson and Herbert was home. They were talking about us. They came home and no dinner. "Three womens at the camp and nothing to eat," I heard them say.

So, I said, "Give us a pan. We'll give you something to eat."

"What you guys do?" he said. "What you kill moose for? Who's going to haul it?"

Madeline said, "Quit talking too much. We never killed no moose."

They brought out a pan. So I dumped my packsack in there. Nobody didn't say anything.

Then Madeline made me walk behind the tent and clean blood off my feet with butcher knife. Her girls was in there and they're not supposed to see it. She brought out some water for me to wash with. Then she take that water away from where we walk. Oh dear, all that trouble. Then she brought out my jeans and made me change outdoors so the girls wouldn't see. And she cleaned my boots up good. I took them off outdoors and hang them outdoors.

Oh my, they talked till about three o'clock in the morning that night. Johnson would get through with one story, then Herbert would start with another one. They had a big feast. They put all the goodies in the oven and the mens had a really good, good something to eat. The next day we went out and took the picture when we're having tea. Just that big head on me that's all. And the gun that I killed it with. Five shots and it killed him. And I couldn't kill nothing with it. We couldn't hit nothing with it. It was just like Papa's words.

Papa's Words

Papa said, "At least have a pocket knife in your parka pocket or take an ax with you." Because I used to just walk. Then I'd come home late at night. When I don't come home, they turned my dog loose and she'd follow me and bring me home.

Papa said there was one time when he was a little boy and they were all hungry. They were always hungry. These two uncles went hunting in spring

Madeline Solomon, Johnson Toby, Herbert Solomon standing over the bear Altona shot, 1949.

time after the water runs up the Koyukuk and up the Kateel. There was certain things the womens couldn't eat so they were hungry. They were looking for spruce hen, rabbits, anything.

So these two brothers seen a rabbit and they couldn't hit it. They didn't think nothing of it. They left their canoe and went over the portage and then they seen some ducks and shoot at those. And those days, they were really careful about their shells. They ration those. It's got to be good shot, otherwise they don't use it.

So his brother caught up with him and said, "You kill anything?"

"No, this gun, there's something wrong with the gun." They looked at it and nothing wrong with it, but they couldn't hit nothing with it. So the youngest brother said, "Let's go back to the canoe. There's something wrong. We'll go in the canoe. Then we'll see him." So they went back to the canoe, went up this creek and into the lake and sure enough, there was a bear. They shot and killed it.

When they came back and told the people about it, it never surprise them. Their father said, "That's the way it is. Anytime you're going to kill a bear, or bear will surprise you. With that gun you'll never kill nothing because he's already sent for it. That's their spirit. The bear already called for that gun and you can't kill nothing with it. It's for him."

I always try to remember that. And here I wasted a whole box and a half for one rabbit and about a dozen chickens. And never killed it. That's what made me happy when I think about Papa's words. So I told Madeline about this story. Oh, she heard about it, but she believed in the old fashioned way that woman's not supposed to kill those things. Oh, I kill anything that moves.

Chapter Six: Life With Dago Kid

Seventeen Years Old

It was springtime and Kokrine people came out to Ruby from spring camp. When I came home everybody was sitting in the front room of my folks. All talking. I don't know what they were talking about. I was in the kitchen. I was going to make bread when I heard Papa said, "Ohhhhh, no!" They were having a meeting. They were drinking, but nobody was drunk. They was just having a drink and sit there talking. I didn't know it was all about me.

Then I hear Papa said to his sister, "Oh no. You people is not going to talk me into it anymore." His youngest sister, they used to live at Kokrine. "I'm just going to leave everything up to her."

"Oh, you're spoiling her," they said.

He said, "Oh yes, I do. She's my favorite daughter. And what you people do? You put all these medicine people together and you come down here and took her when she's barely took her diaper off." Gee, he talk rough to his sister. He usually don't. Then he said, "Then what will happen to her? We'll see about that. We'll see what will happen to her."

That was all that was said. So I sneaked down the back stairs and went over to DeVane's. I was working for him in his store at the waterfront. They told me to go to hotel room and just stay there till tomorrow and go back to work. I wanted to quit right there. Are they going to help me? Are they going to say to come on over and stay at their place? They never thought, I guess. They never know how serious it was.

So I went to next door. There was a clothing store there. An elderly lady, Mrs. Anne Hoffman, was running it. She says, "Oh, you wandering around? What's the matter, your folks drinking?" I told her, "Not only my folks, but

84

the people from Kokrine is all over there. They're having a great big meeting." She ask me right away what's the meeting about. I said, "About me."

She talked to me for a long time. She wasn't married. I stayed with her two days and nobody didn't know where I went. I didn't go back to work. Then my uncle, Ivan Hardluck, came down from Kokrines and went over to DeVane's. Asked DeVane if I'd been around.

Uncle Ivan and Dago Kid was good friends. They been friends ever since they started talking English to one another. And we know Dago Kid since we were kids. He used to come down and we used to feed his dogs. Then he'd bring us cookies, and bag of candy, quite a big pay. We always liked him. He was a guy, parents would trust him. He just didn't like that first husband at all. Because he seen us growing up down there since we were small kids. And he was real good to me that winter. He talked to me and always look after the boy. Everybody ask me what I'm going to do. Right away I shut up and just walk away from them. After being with that terrible man I didn't want anything like that.

So one day I went home. I washed up and changed clothes. I had enough of that hiding. I thought, oh well, I'll go back to work. I got to live. I got to take care of the boy. He was over there with my folks. When I got home, nobody was there. They all left, I guess. Papa never say nothing. Mamma talked, sure, that, "You're going to turn into something else if you don't look out." I never told them where I'd been.

I went back to work and Dago Kid was playing pool. He said, "Ah ha! Did you get lost?"

"Yep," I said.

"Why don't you get lost with me?" That was the first time he ever said anything to me that's out of the way. I never said nothing. I went over there on the other side where I was working, clothing store. That pool table was in the same building, way back. And he thought he said the greatest thing in the

She said, "Leave her alone. If she's going to marry him I'll help her." So she give me her dress.

Tom DeVane said, "You just take two people and don't say anything to nobody. Just go down there at the what-you-call-'ems office. Go ahead and do your job if you can stand it."

I said, "I think he'll understand me."

He says, "Sister, you're making a mistake."

"Well, my folks made a mistake by giving me away when I was still on the bottle." I walked out. I went home. Mamma was still mad. Papa wasn't, so I said, "I'm going to get married Pop."

"To Dago Kid," he said. He know all the time. Maybe he talked to him. I don't know. The only time I was ever alone with Dago Kid, we had the little boy with us. I went to the fish net with him. But Dago Kid never said anything out of the way. Never said boo to me. Never said nothing.

Papa grabbed hold of me and he cried. Held me in his arms and he cried. Then Mamma came in. She said, "I wish I'd know, really know, what you are doing." Then I went and loved her up.

I said, "Just remember that you give me away when I was still a baby. I have nobody right now since Thomas is gone." They both start crying. I walked out. Went up to my sister, Rose. That was her home, where the preachers are now. I told her, "Come with me. I'm going to get married." So Rose and

Photo by Altona Brown. Altona Brown Collection

Altona, Dago Kid and Madeline Notti. "That's Madeline's snowshoes. Taken maybe in the 30's about 20 miles below Poorman on our trapline at one of our relief cabins. Our little boy was at home with Mary Dean. You can see the cord and button I'm holding to take that picture. I took lots that way."

Alexander Brown otherwise known as "Dago Kid". "I don't know when that was taken. Maybe before I was born!" Altona Brown Collection

"My girl Marie and old man (Dago Kid) cooking salmon for dogfood. Must be year '27, we cut her hair like boy and she cried. I'm out on the cutting raft. 800 fish on that table behind them."

Rosie Burk

Dago Kid, age 12 in Washington.

Altona in the 30's. "That's the year my boy got chewed up and I came to Fairbanks. You notice they took the birthmark off my face in the photograph."

Altona with her niece and nephew, Mamie Burk Allen and Billy Burk Jr. in Nenana.

Altona with her son Buster at age 2.

Burk went down to the Commissioner's Office and we got married. We didn't even have a party or nothing. We went from there to the fish camp. Little old log cabin. You know he couldn't even talk, he surprised himself. He was, I guess, over forty. I must have been seventeen. Well, we were married twenty-one years.

Enjoying Work

That same fall we got married, he bought this house. I don't know exactly whose house it was. I thought it was George Armstrong's because Mom went and visit them. She used to always make boots or birchbark baskets for them people. And when they were leaving, we went up to see them. I never dreamed that it was going to be my house. It used to be a beautiful place. But you know, it's old now.

He didn't bother me. He just let me grow into my home, which is a

Altona Brown Collection

"My home when they first moved it from up the hill, maybe 1927. Doc Frost was watching it."

wonderful thing. I didn't know what life is all about. But he's the one that I learned from. Sounds fantastic doesn't it? But it's true. When you don't have education, nothing to look forward to, just go ahead and work like a dog. I started to think that way.

We worked together right from the beginning. He was a fisherman. He didn't do much about trapping at that time. But he was the marshall most of the time. And he was raising dogs for McKinley Park and the Road Commission. That's a lot of dogs. You have to raise a lot in order to get the best ones out of them. Every fall we had about twenty-five to thirty-five pups. And I was the one that broke them in. Oh, I really know how to talk dog language.

One time I was big with baby and coming down the hill. You know how steep it is here in Ruby. We had dog barn over there across the street from the church, on the other side of Bob Kennedy. It was a long building with dog boxes on each side like stalls for horses. At the back was a 12' x 12' room with frozen fish on one side and hay on the other side. We just let the puppies loose in there to feed themselves on frozen fish. So here I was big with the baby and I come all the way down that hill with twenty-one dogs. Half pups and some grown dogs. I was holding the brake. I never think about I might get hurt or something. As I go down any men standing around would grab here and there on the line and try to slow them down. They used to get a kick out of that many dogs.

Usually I'd hook up about eleven dogs. My brother Rocker would go with me. After I kill dogs, pups, in the harness, he didn't want to go with me anymore. Because the third time they deliberately drag on the harness, they're no good. They don't want to work no more. So I'd kill them. So I raised them and I broke them in. I started them at two or three months old and Dago Kid would sell them at eight or nine months, take them across country to Ophir or McGrath. He'd leave here with about twenty-five or thirty dogs, then sell it. He'd keep about eleven dogs to come back with and have the mail carrier take more dogs to the people buying them. Dad was good at that. He let people try out the team. Maybe he'd go out with them from Cripple to McGrath.

One time I raised half-labrador dogs. They were coal black, shiny, nice looking dogs. Somebody give me the dog that was going to have pups so I brought it in from Poorman. Seven dogs. Oh, they were nice. They take me everywhere. He took that cross-country and sold it to a guy from Ophir. Like I said, he'd leave here with two teams, twenty-five to thirty dogs. Big dogs, pulling big sled. He'd be on gee-pole. Haul a lot of fish that way. And what he don't feed out there, he sell that. Oh, he was a gambler. He'd sell anything.

Most of the dogs we raised for the Road Commissioner at McKinley Park. They used them to maintain the place like they do with airplane and car right now. Use them to haul people, haul stuff. They maintained the road with dog team. They must have had tourists in those days. So I raised the dogs for them and break them in. I was the boss of those dogs.

He would be busy with the marshalls while I'm taking care of pups. He had contract to haul the prisoners and crazy

Altona with Ralph Nelson's dogs at Poorman in the early '30's.

"This side of Poorman. three dogteams — Bergman, me and mail team. That's the way we used to come in middle of May."

people. Haul them from here on the Iditarod Trail and then go to Holy Cross. Or he would pick them up at Iditarod, Flat, bring them through here to Fairbanks. Sometimes he don't come home at all and take them cross-country to McGrath and through Nenana. Haul the marshall and the prisoners.

It was a long time till the airplanes come along. Even after the airplanes we were still fishing for McKinley Park dog food, raising dogs till he died. We put up ten tons of dry fish for them summertime. The boat used to land at our fish camp and pick them up. We worked hard, real hard. But I didn't think I was working hard. I was enjoying it.

Cutting Fish

Summertime I don't get up until ten-thirty. I sleep. They don't dare wake me up. He shoo the children, shut the door in the bedroom and I sleep. He got to rest his machine. So when I wake up I get up, prepare dinner for him, wash the dishes, and go down and start cutting fish. I walk down to the cutting raft and, eeee! All the fish, thousands of them, all looking at me. I

Altona and Dago Kid's fish camp in Ruby circa 1929.

Big Joe with pipe, right to left: Leo Marie, Altona holding fish tail, Ida Marie and Tom Marie on Altona and Dago Kid's fish raft, 1929 in Ruby.

94

don't think nothing of it. And those salmons were big those days. I don't know why they're not that big now. Maybe they're catching them so much down at the mouth of the Yukon, they don't let them grow.

I just cut and split them, cut the bones off and make a big pile. Daddy, my husband, used to make the strips. He wouldn't let me strip them. That's too hard," he said. Sometimes I cut strips if he was way up on the fourth tier in the smokehouse. That would take a long time putting fish strips up there and if the sun hits the fish, I have to cut them.

Papa was always there too, cutting fish with Dad and me. Sometimes Dad go someplace, go start dinner or something. Then Papa's the only one on the raft with me. He wouldn't let me stay on the raft alone. No I was Papa's girl. That's why I was such a crybaby, I guess.

Papa teach me how to cut fish when I was a little girl down at camp. I cried because I couldn't cut the fish head off. I was just little when I started cutting fish. Then he said, "No." Then I'd stop. He'd let me figure out how. Why did he stop me. He never look at me. He'd go hang his head cutting fish and I keep waiting. I turn the fish over and I looked at his fish. Then I see what I was doing wrong. I had to figure it out myself. He wouldn't tell me.

He show me how to sharpen knife then too. Just touch it up on a greasy dry pole. Fish pole. You know, at the cutting table. Sharpen it up real good on steel first. Then touch it up on pole or hard surface. It keeps the edge. I have to learn by looking. And he always had this leaf tobacco. He always doctor me up with that when I cut myself.

Sometimes we had 1,800 or 3,000 fish a day. Those days we have to go back to work after supper and work till nine o'clock. But most of the day I don't take break. Oh, they'll bring me cold root beer. But I don't like to stop. I try to finish my job, no matter how tired I get. Just like walking home on snowshoes when you walk all day long cleaning traps and have few animals in your packsack. I try to make it home, into the house and get a fire going before I pass out. Fishing is same way.

That's the way I was since I was small. Because I was in bed so much, sick. When I'm up, I'm tearing the house down. Even at fish camp. We're busy, and we have big house with wooden floor. Just as clean as could be. You could eat off the floor.

I don't really know the fastest I could cut but I know it would be 120 an hour anytime. But when I was mad, I don't know how many I could cut. One time Dad round up bunch of people. I don't know nothing about it. I guess they were bow-wowwing over there in Carl Bohn's store about how fast I could cut fish. They got in an argument so jumped in Henry Romensted's boat and come on up. Henry was bootlegger over there at Melozi. We used to take care of him all the time. He finally died over there all by himself. Mice ate him up, poor thing. It was during the ice running in the falltime. My, how I hate mice.

Papa and I was still cutting fish. There was another lady that was cutting fish with us, but she got tired. Soon as she saw this whole bunch of men coming, she went to the shore. They all line up on the other side of the table. The table was long with boat under it. About sixteen feet long. Long as the raft. Everything goes in the boat,

Thousands of fish on the racks. Workers on the raft cut steady, Altona cut 120 fish an hour at her peak.

Loading up 10 tons of dog salmon at Altona and Dago Kid's fish camp. The fish were bound for Fort Yukon. Circa 1937.

96

blood, water, heads, guts, backbones. Then we take it across the river, reverse it and it all goes out the trap door.

They were all looking at me. Watch me cut the head off, split them, gut them, see how many scores I made and how fast I sling it onto that rack behind me. I didn't like them watching, but I didn't pay any attention to them. I don't see nobody when I'm working. So I was cutting away. It's just automatic. But someway I touched my coveralls and shirt with the knife and sliced my arm.

Gee whiz, I was bleeding, blood was pouring out. Papa looked over, took his gloves off, rinsed his hands and go in his pocket. He took out this roll of leaf tobacco, put in in his mouth and come over to me. He slap that wet tobacco on my arm and tell me to grab it, hold it, but my hand was still fishy.

Dad started hollering. He come down and said, "Don't touch it with that fishy hand!" He got scared. Wanted to take me downtown. Papa just grab it and held it there for twenty minutes, wrap it up. In four days there was only scar there. He did that with my hand too. I was on the cache and Rose grab hold of my dress and I tumbled over. I fell off and fell right on top of double-bladed ax down there. I cover my face when I fell. The hand in front hit that ax and almost cut the whole thing off. Just the bone. Gee, I would have cut my face. Just a little bitty girl. Papa took it, held it for a while. It's just crooked a little bit now.

Well, after Papa wrap it up, I just roll down my sleeve and started cutting. We had about sixty more to cut. Papa said he'll finish it, but I didn't want him to stay down there all alone. Henry Romensted start bawling them out. He says, "That's not easy working. You guys see what you did? It's all on account of you she cut her arm." They all got off the raft and stand on the beach. There was about six of them. They didn't know what to do. I guess they felt guilty. Here they all come out from the creeks and were having a great time, timing me. They collect their money. My old man won that one. He was gambling all the time. They argue about who cut fish faster. Some say Scotty Clark was. But he cut it too close to the skin. In bad weather all his fish fell down, but then any fish would fall down.

Deliver Babies

I cut 800 fish one day and went home and cooked dinner. Then I washed clothes. And no washer. You do it in a washtub with a washboard. I washed clothes for about four hours I guess and hung them up. Every once in a while I rest. Papa noticed that so he went over to smokehouse and told Dad. He said, "I think your girl is ready to have her baby."

Oh! He got so scared. He said, "Are you sick?" I told him I wasn't. He said, "Come on, get ready. Papa said you're ready to have the baby." We left the camp and come on up here to the house.

I told Dad, "You tell Mrs. Timothy (Agnes Pitka) to come on over and wash dishes for me." We had been here at the house few days before that for the dance. We didn't wash the dishes because we were too sleepy after the dance. We just took off. So she come over. She guessed right away what was wrong. So she come over. You don't tell them right direct. You go round-about in the old fashioned way. That's why I told her, come on over to wash dishes for me.

So she was here to take care of me. But I don't like her hanging around. So I told her, "Why don't you go sweep the floor. It look like it's going to be for a while." So here I was in the bedroom almost all alone when this third baby come along. I called her. September 13, 1932, Alexander "Buster" Brown was born. Seven twenty in the evening. Just like that.

Oh, I help with a lot of babies. I figure it's over 100 I delivered with somebody present. But fifty babies I deliver alone. I delivered one little girl from my cousin. I must have been twenty, a long time ago. And soon as she had it, here comes Mom. She didn't want me to deliver babies. She said, "It's not that easy and you're young. You could pick up something if the people's not clean when you deliver baby. You have to be awful careful. Wash your hands and be careful all the time." She say that because there was lot of TB at that time. It seems like everybody had it.

Afterwards, Mom showed me what to do in the old fashioned way. Like when you take the baby out, you put your finger down his throat. There is a cotton-like mucous, really hard mucous, you have to push down or take out. And another thing she told me was to wipe their eyes right now. When a baby is born and had trouble with the eyes, drop breast milk in it's eyes and down it's nose on both sides. That clears it up. That's the only things she ever told me. From there on I just do it old fashioned way. I always told the doctors how I did it. And when Dr. Dunlap deliver his babies, he puts his finger down it's throat and said, "That's the way Mrs. Brown delivered them."

I can tell when a person's ready to have a baby by the way they act. You don't have to see if they're dilating or anything. Us Indians never did. You can tell. And old fashioned way is sitting up when they deliver. They have their feet under them and sitting up on their knees. That's easy delivery for them I guess. But I deliver all my babies lying down.

And I always tell my people it's nothing to have a baby. It got to come out. You can't carry it forever, and you're hurting. The quicker you get rid of it, the better it is. Which is right.

Trapping

My husband didn't trap until long after we were married. He was too busy. Just about the time he get going, they'll call for him. He didn't like that. When the airplane got here, that's when he start trapping. I didn't know about trapping. He couldn't learn from me.

About year '26 or '27, we went out cross-country to Ophir. It was my cousin, Bergman Wholecheese, Dad, and the baby, Marie. She was two years old. My brother Claude and Aunt Winifred's husband were there for little while and went back with mail carrier. We camped eleven miles below Ophir all spring. It was a nice camp. I sit in the tent at this two big lake. The beaver is out there flapping their tails and having a great time. I just sat in the tent and watch it. Watch the baby. Never think about killing anything.

Dad and Bergman was trapping. They had two canoe. That was fast water and you had to have someone with you all the time. They could shoot beaver that time too. When Dad came home they brought an otter. They skinned it and left it there, went hunting. I took it and slinged it on a pile of willows. Willows I had cut so in the front of the tent was just clear and beautiful. Bear come by the tent and got that otter. Never paid attention to me. I talk to it. I ask what he's doing, how far he's going. He just mind his own business and walk away. Dad come home and I tell him about it. He said, "There's that gun. You know how to shoot? But I didn't want to kill it if he's not doing anything wrong.

All spring it was like that. I don't want to kill anything. The beaver was all over in the lake, in the morning about four o'clock. I stay up for it and watch them because the men are out every night hunting beaver and rats. Until they got the boat built. All they bought was nails at Ophir. They whipsaw lumber and built those canoes to go home. They planned it out. I was too young and dumb. I always stay home, sew and cook, all except breakfast. He always cook breakfast. I made fancy trim for my parka that spring.

When I started trapping, I didn't want nobody to show

Altona hunting with Andy Wholecheese.

me how. I wanted to learn on my own. That time I teach myself I just chase my old man. He leave me home lot of times and he take off. But I'd be sitting there sewing, thinking... what did he see without me? I took off. He didn't think I could follow him, that's a long ways to just a little this side of McGrath.

I went all alone out there on the trail. It was in between the mail. At that time they was carrying mail with dogs. I was in between so I'd be all alone on the trail. My goodness, that's long ways. It's just twenty miles this side to Ophir. He was trapping on Folger Creek. Gee, I scared him. He almost shot me.

In front of John Walker's store at Long Creek town. L-r: John Walker, Altona, Sig Wiig. "That's the way we used to come in, in the spring, no snow. The sled is the mail carrier's, Sig Wiig. I came in behind him with my dogs."

He was in this little old dark cabin cooking lunch. It's a cut bank next to it and he didn't see my dogs when I came up. And I had this parka on with nice ruff. He thought I was wolf. He didn't think anybody would visit him. He was glad to see me although he was scared to death. I went out there long enough to get my limit. Then I turn around and come home. But he made sure that I go behind the mail team.

After that the government let you shoot beaver for two years, I guess. Then they shut it down again and let you trap and snare them. We trapped over there at Hogan's on the South Fork of the Innoko mostly. Hardly any ice there. It's running wild all the time. It's way up at the head where we used to trap. You could see right down where they been and sink your trap down there. In no time at all you catch them, and otter. I used to like to trap.

I was trying to skin them. I was doing a pretty good job on it. Papa always showed me how. He showed me how to skin a marten through the mouth. Just cut around the mouth with real sharp knife. And you slip the skin by it's neck over the shoulder and pull it down. When you get to the arms, just pull it out and cut it's nails off. It's fast, clean and no flesh, nothing on it.

Must be 1929, trapping was so good. Lots of fox and fox was high. Cross fox were $150.00 and red fox were up to fifty, sixty dollars a piece. Before that it was just two and a half. I must have had thirty and he had lots. I caught a lynx too and four mink. I just got crazy that one winter. We just made a killing. We left early too, in February. That's the year we went Outside. Just like a drunken sailor.

Altona with her husband Dago Kid at their home cabin at the head of Agate Creek. They got 73 marten that trip. Notice the string Altona is pulling to take the photo. "The parka border behind me is the one I made in 1927 when I didn't hunt."

Our daughter, Marie, was five years old then. He took us from here to Nenana with dog team when we were going Outside. It was a nice trip. We left Ruby with eleven dogs. Dad sold them in Nenana. We had the time of our life. They all know him in all the villages. And everybody made party for us. Of course, he was always shine at the gambling table. We went to Seattle to visit his folks. Went on the boat from Seward to Seattle. His dad was already dead. Just his mom and sisters and brothers.

Gee, Papa try to talk me out of that trip. He felt bad. He said, "You should go up the Kateel where your grandfather used to live off the country Why don't you fly up there?" But I sure had nice time on that trip. I had nice picture taken of Marie in Seattle at one of those fancy studios. Real nice one.

When we come back from Seattle in May to Fairbanks, there was too much water on the river. Dad don't want us on the river so we come back to Ruby with airplane. We got back here a week ahead of Dad. He and Old Man Billy Burk left Nenana to bring the dogs down for the camp. They traveled with

Dago Kid, Marie and Altona in front of Shel Wettach's store in Ruby, 1927. "We just came back from Innoko when we went from Ophir."

102

forty-two dogs from Nenana to Ruby, and wet! The day they got here is when the big fire broke out downtown Ruby. Two streets went with all those fancy buildings.

Well, at the time of that fire there was a lot of vacant buildings. I don't know how many people from here, the whole mining camps people were gone. Whole bunch of them on that ship that sunk out at sea, the *Sophia*. So after the fire, the shops moved into the vacant buildings. Only the guys from the restaurant and some clothing store left on account of the fire.

Food on the Trapline

We usually cooked up brown beans. Just cook a whole bucket full and then drain it out, put them in a four sack. Now they have that plastic bag, but we didn't have that. So we put it in a flour sack and freeze it. Then we'd take moose hamburgers or diced meat and fat cut up together, keep that where it's frozen. And when you come to the camp you put frying pan on. When it gets hot, throw those meat and beans in there. It almost makes its own gravy. Beans and meat. There you got a whole meal.

One time we went up, over head of

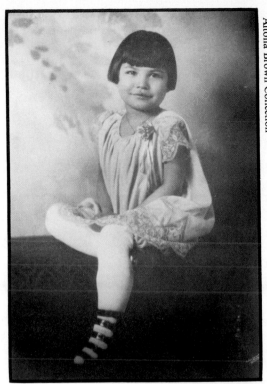

Altona's daughter Marie age 5 in Seattle, 1929.

Rosie and Burk

"The big 1929 fire in Ruby that took two streets. That's Doc Frost in front. We just got back from Outside."

Sulatna. It was 1931. Year after Mamma died. I stayed up there with Papa up the Deer Creek all winter. Way up on the other side of bridge toward Twin Buttes. Papa head out already and I was just waiting for my husband to come cross country and pick me up. Finally going home. I was going to pick up my traps and my husband said, "I'll go with you."

"Gee, that's a steep hill. It's just like going up to the Ruby cemetery someplaces. If you're game enough, okay. Let's go," I told him.

So we went packing on snowshoes. First we put little block of wood in the stove. I put two little pieces of meat in dutch oven, season it and put half full of water. Put that on top of the stove. Figure I'll make the gravy when I come home. It won't take long to come back. Crazy fool.

He just made it to the top of the hill and ask me how far to go. I told him we have to make a big circle all the way around. He asks if I want to go. He would pick up my traps if I want to go back and finish stew. No, I want to go.

Coming home it got real dark. He asked me which way to go from here. I said, "Oh, you walk behind and I'll walk ahead." And as we were coming down the side of the hill the moon come up. It was shining against the hill real nice. And here, two chickens flew up! I said, "Dad, you catch your breath?"

"What you mean catch my breath?"

I said, "There's two chicken up there. Can you see them?" He had a .22 special.

He said, "Okay, you shoot the one and I'll shoot the other. Two-to-one, I'll get it." We start to argue.

"How do you know you're going to shoot it?" I tell him. "Okay, one kiss to two kisses." That's what we always bet when we're hunting. So I shot and down come the

"My husband and our little boy Buster with his dog. About 1937, home cabin at head of Agate, tributary to Novi."

bird. He shot, but we didn't even see the bird, didn't even see it fly. We say that's not even bird and started laughing. I tell him, "You're the one to pay the bill." So we rolled around on the snow for a while and I went and got my chicken.

We take our time and walk and visit going down the hill. I plucked the chicken while it's warm. That's easy time to pluck it, never tear no skin that way.

We finally got down there to the house and he lit the Coleman lamp. He was going to start the fire and I opened the little dutch oven. Two little ashes in there! How crazy. I should have known it was going to get hot. Good thing we had that chicken because we're out of grub and just ready to go home.

Used to be a lot of people and a lot of buildings around this country. Not like now, they're just all growed over or burned down. Cross country, Poorman and Placerville, Timber and Flat was all in the same area. Then Long Creek and Spruce Creek and Sulatna was all in another area. Fourteen Mile was a beautiful roadhouse, beautiful log building. I remember when the army boys come up in helicopters and raid it few years back. And the one in Long Creek was the Goose House. It was a big beautiful hotel. It had two stories and I don't know how many rooms. It was so beautiful. And down below they had a roadhouse and poolroom and store all in one building.

Long Creek was a big place. They hauled everything in by horses and dogs to build that place. I think it was bigger than Poorman. Really, so many people. At that time we'd come up for Fourth of July. I don't know why those people just up and went. Nice home and they just up and go after the gold rush is over. Leave everything behind. Isn't that crazy? I never heard of such a thing. Well, people pick all those places over now.

Goose House is where I'd go when they dance at my house for a week or ten days. Dancing and poker. When I get tired of them I hook up my dogs and head out. Johnny Walker would go tie up my dogs and I go to bed. I sleep for forty-eight hours. Just trying to catch sleep. I stay up too long dancing and visiting.

Those days people don't clear out. Most of them stay all winter. They cut wood and haul it all winter for their boilers. All old fashioned equipment. They don't have cats. They have to work the ground with boilers and dig holes, dig the ground in winter.

Twice in the summertime we'd go out to Long Creek. They invited us out when the boys cleaned up. Oh, we'd drive out in little old car, maybe Ford, then the Dodge came. The road was rough and soupy. So we go out and raise hell for two or three days. We had a good time. He play cards and I dance. I used to love to dance. The mining camp people, Tellison's crew, was all musicians. They had fiddlers, guitar and accordian. After work you could just lay out there under the tree and listen to them. Oh, it was so beautiful. And when they have a party, it's all kinds of dance. Schottish is what I really love to do. And they have two step and square dance. Oh, we had fun. And Dad played cards.

Now, we had a contest there and Oliver Anderson and I was the one that topped it all. We danced for fourteen hours straight. We are still dancing when they quit playing. They tried to tire us out but we wouldn't.

I dance all night without even changing shoes. I used to wear high heel for dancing. My husband think I have to look like a doll. He'd wear overalls, wouldn't dress up. But he always want me to dress up and wear the good clothes. I had velvet dress one time and another one was crepe satin and then chiffon, black one and beige one. They dress up a lot those days for parties.

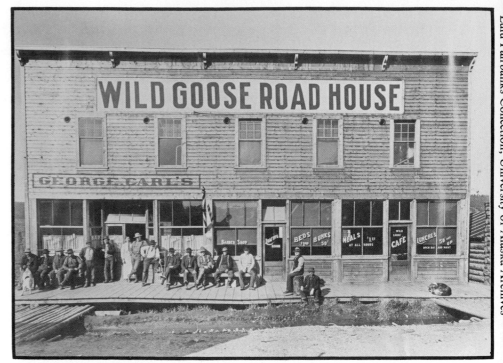
Long Creek roadhouse, 1912.

4th of July Egg Race at Long Creek, 1916.

Long Creek, 1980.

Old Mrs. Sturdevant's bunkhouse at Long Creek, once a thriving business has lost it's luster. 1980.

"Used to be a lot of people and a lot of buildings around this country. Not like now, they're just all growed over...." Old woodstove at Long Creek, 1980.

107

Gambling

We didn't have no bank account or nothing. Never did. He make all kinds of money but, gee, his hands are just itchy. He wants to get in a poker game with it. He really cured himself one time. He went downtown and never came back till the next day. Then he went in the kitchen, washed his face, changed his shirt and went out again. $2300.00 he lost. Just like that.

I went out and ask Tom DeVane, "How much money does it entail?" Just then Jim Dodson landed on the river with his airplane so I asked him if he got room for me. He said sure, so I run home, packed up a suitcase, run down, got in the plane and was gone. I was so mad. I went to Fairbanks and Anchorage. I was gone for

Altona in Seattle, 1929. "I still have that muskrat belly coat." Altona Brown Collection

Sherborn Avenue, Long Creek City 1912. Notice the sign for telephone pay station. Telephone service was widespread along the Yukon.

about a month. Back in Fairbanks I met Jim Dodson at the Nordale Hotel. He said, "You ready to go home? Your old man was looking for you. He want to take off for the beaver trapping." I told him I'm ready to go now. And he looked at me and said, "You had a good time?"

I said, "No. I was lonesome all the time I was gone." I couldn't stay away from him. I often think about it after he was gone. I think about the time I would get mad and stay away from him. I feel terrible. Don't ever try that.

When I went home he was up there at the schoolhouse sawing wood. He had contract to saw the wood and haul it with dogs. He came down to the house and says, "Oh, you come back?" We never quarrel, anything. I was afraid to. When I do get mad and say a few things to him, he feels bad. I just can't stand it.

One time I went on a strike and didn't go to the fish camp. No matter how much I was hurting, I wouldn't go. I caught him with my cousin. I said, "Go get your fancy girls. They can cut fish for you." Jealous is a terrible thing. It's poison. It's a good thing I didn't start fighting with him. I think I'd kill him. It's funny how, when you love a person so much. And when they disappoint you, you are hurt, right to the core.

It's a good thing I didn't haul off and get mad. I'm awful when I'm mad. I'm mad all the way through. Even my bones get mad. Papa always told me to go out in the woods and hunt. "Take your little gun and go out in the woods and hunt. You'll feel better." I always do. And the animals that the other women don't kill. That's what made me feel happy.

But mostly we work together. After I went on the strike that summer he didn't beg me to go to camp. After while I get over it. Get right back to working hard. Gee, I sure miss him when he's gone.

Buster and Altona. "That's the year I went on strike. I was sick at heart and stayed home." 1937 or 1938.

109

Chapter Seven: Altona On Her Own

Raising Kids

My husband was at fish camp hooking up dogs when he had heart attack. He got through that one so we sent him to Fairbanks. I couldn't come in because we had forty-six dogs to take care of and everyone was gone out of Ruby, everybody trapping. So he saw Dr. Schaible and took off. Here I thought he was with the doctor all that time in Fairbanks but he took off to Circle playing poker, for whole week. He got back to Fairbanks and one day sat down on the chair and that was it. He was gone. December 18, 1943. Marie and I brought back his body and buried him. $700 to bring him on airplane. I never dreamed he'd leave me. Oh, I miss him. People never knowed.

Then I took his dogs and my dogs together and went downriver to Galena with Marie. We had nine dogs. He wasn't there and they don't care to eat, just starve themselves after he was gone. They lay down and when you're not watching, they howl. Howl, howl. Terrible. About twenty days after, my youngest brother, Lincoln Antoski, died down in Galena. He's the father of that adopted daughter, Pearl.

When Dad died Buster was 11. Pearl, the baby we adopted, was a year old. I had to raise those kids. Marie was a young woman. Must be nineteen. After that trip to Galena, I started right to work at roadhouse. It was at the corner where the theater used to be. I worked hard too, all day long, cooking for Millie and Wise Beese and them.

Dago Kid. "He didn't like having his picture taken. That's our trapline cabin."

It was sad. It was the first time I ever cooked breakfast. When I was home, Papa always cooked breakfast. Dad did too. And cruel as he was, the first old guy that I was married to used to get up and cook breakfast. I worked too hard all day long.

Then I worked at another roadhouse across the street with Mamie Wick for a long time. Eight o'clock in the morning to eleven o'clock every night, worked all day long, eight dollars. That's all for cooking, washing dishes and take care of the kitchen. And there was a lot of people staying at that place that time. There was engineers, builders, cat train, whole bunch of people working on the FAA buildings. She made plenty money. I was a slave, but I didn't care. I had to work. I'd rather work than put up with anybody, some man to take care of me.

A year or two later, Marie had Bobo. That's Claude Keough, my first grandson. They stay with me because Marie was working down at the store, bookkeeping. I took them away from Leo, the boy's father. I told him, "Come back and get her when you build a house for her."

"Me, brother Lincoln and cousin Luana Nichols. Around year '40 at Galena when my brother got sick."

Playing guitars in Galena, 1944. Standing l-r: Bessie Wholecheese, Old Man Leo Captain and wife Sophie Captain. Back: Behind the sailor hat is Francis Williams, Joe Wholecheese, Andy Williams.

"At Galena, we were going to the graveyard."

111

And I have to pay for my boy's school when he started high school. First Buster went to Edgecumbe and then Seward. I pay for his fare back and forth. I done without lot of things that I was used to at the beginning. But it was alright, he got his education. Then he started to go to college at Los Angeles. He was holding down two jobs and his wife helped him. He learn to be dental technician and make teeth. I have a partial made by him. He quit that and learn how to build airplanes when he got killed. He was building planes and a friend of his picked him up after work. In twenty minutes they were gone. Both of them. Their airplane blowed up. His wife buried him down there two hours before I landed. Broke my heart. No wonder I had heart trouble. But I lived through it.

My girls went to school too. Marie went to Eklutna. Pearl went to Holy Cross when she was just a little girl. She was the only one that went down there besides my aunt. Pearl was just five years old when I sent her down. She stayed down there four years. I was working steady all that time, and then I was awfully sick. That's when I had a heart attack and they didn't think I was going to pull through. The first big one was '53. I noticed that everytime I worked, I got sick.

I raised those kids alone most of the time, the boy and my adopted daughter. They come out alright. And I never had much time for them because I'm working all the time. Everybody help take care of them. Johnny May really helped me lots with the boy. Like if someone thinks they're doing something wrong, they say something. They try to explain it to them. Help them out. I do too, but everybody helped.

In those days, very few troubles people had. It's nowadays that they get into mischief and do things. And in those days there was hardly any suicide. I don't know why there's so much now, it's so common for young people. Maybe now nobody explains things to them. And when they get disgusted it's the only easy way out for them. It seems like when they get discouraged that's the first thing they do. It's because they don't know. They don't know things will get better. They don't know no other way.

You know, long time ago when people get mad they used to tell them to take off and go in the woods and kill big animal or something. Well, there was no law against it at the time, seasons and all that. They say kill big animal and that takes it out of their system. Like bear, you get happy when you kill that one. I do. I think my troubles are over. The only thing womens used to do with bear is pull up their dress and show them it's woman. I don't think that works, but I never learned that until I was full grown woman out with Jenny. But you have to explain things while kids are small. Start real early. Before five or six. Otherwise, they're too old already. Just little bitty guys get into all kind of mischief. Chewing tobacco, smoking something, or drinking together. Just kids. I don't like to see it. It makes me feel bad. What's the use to have children if you're not going to raise them right?

Sewing

I made money with sewing too. Ever since I was married to that awful man, I tan mooseskin and tan work moccasin, snowshoe moccasin. Only $2.50 for those wrap-around work moccasin. I buy groceries with it. Me and my sister been sewing since we're little girls. We watch what Mom does and learned by ourselves. She'd give us junk to work with, play with. When we get stuck we ask her. That's how we learn. And pretty soon we have to make our own clothes, boots, parkas, mitts and all those winter things.

I used to sew anything that people order that I can do. I'd make boots out of calfskins or sealskins with hard bottom, caribou legging boots, marten hats. I used to get orders from all over. I liked to do my own tanning. I don't like that chemical tan from Outside. It's cold and don't last very long. I

Altona and Luana McQueston making tea at Yuki Island.

On the beach at Ruby, 1934. L-r: Mary Dean holding Buster, Jennie Jacob holding Regina Pitka, Belena Jacob Williams, Marie Brown, Lilly Henry and daughter Luana.

113

don't know what it is but it's that way with the mooseskin and the beaver. I tanned my own mooseskin until a few years ago. But I had light stroke and that slow me down. Still, I try to do little bit. I push myself. I can't stand to just sit around. Have to do something! But I can't sew anymore for sale. My eyes are bad for fancy work. I just barely sew for my grandchildren.

Hunting with Dolly

Of course, all those years alone I can't just wait around for meat to come to me. I have to keep up with my hunting and do little bit of trapping. Fishing was the same way. I had good partner too. I really enjoyed going out with Dolly Yrjana. When Dolly and I went hunting we didn't go in a boat, we went in a car. The only time she hollered at me was when we saw brown bear out at Seven Mile.

I thought it was moose. Gee, it was big. We were picking berries. Well, we didn't exactly pick berries. We just get off the road and look around. And I said, "Dolly, is there a moose down there?" She took out her gun, .306. I just had .22 special, my special gun I always take with me. So Dolly gets ready with her gun. That moose turns broadside and, goodness, it didn't look like moose, it's legs were too short.

I said, "Dolly, it that moose?"

"I guess so," she said. "What do you think?"

"Oh no, that's a brown bear!" When I said that the sound carried off that jeep and make the tin vibrate. Just like that! The bear was gone. He just leaped for the woods. Boy, could they move fast.

Altona sewing fancy calfskin trim at her home in Ruby, 1980.

Dolly said, "Get in the car!" I told Dolly we should look for his tracks. "Oh, the hell with his tracks, let's get out of here!" The only time she ever hollered at me.

We were fishing one time. I thought this time she was going to get mad, but it wasn't my fault. We were fishing and it's in my boat. So we just left the fishwheel with boat load of fish. It's at that bluff below the camp. I told her to shove it out. You know, shove the boat off the fishwheel when we're tied. So she shoved it out.

Well, it looked like the boat was going to take in water so I started the kicker. Well, we

Dolly Yrjana and Altona in Ruby, 1980.

went upriver just above the wheel and, doggone, if the kicker didn't stop. That fishwheel is so close and it's just like we were going to break into it. Dolly start to get scared and I'm telling her to "shove it out." We were just about to hit the poles when the kicker started. Oh boy, I bet she done a lot of praying.

I thought she would get mad but when we got up to the camp, she turned around and looked at me, she smile. She said, "Thank God it was you." She hug me. Nobody didn't get excited or nothing. We done a lot of things together. We done it hard too, worked hard. But we never argued. Never got mad or nothing. Oh, she talk rough, and I talk rough, and we don't mean anything. She was good hunting partner, we were.

Only place I didn't take her is downriver. I meant to take her down to where we used to live. Oh, we went way up the river. We'd get inside those creeks, then she'd say, "That's enough now, let's go back." I don't know why she was afraid of bear. They don't do nothing but run away. It's quite a while that we were out the last time. She broke her ankle twice on the same foot and since then has slowed down altogether.

In the falltime we used to go out hunting with her husband, Albert. One time he talked so big. Here, coming home from Fifteen Mile, moose was right ahead of us. Raining cats and dogs. Albert jumped out and shot at it about five times. Nothing happened. I don't know why he didn't kill that one. So big and so close! He always had funny little stories about those things. Because I always tease him. And then when Dolly and I go out alone we never killed any.

When I killed that moose out on the road at Twenty-six Mile in '76, she said she was wishing that she was with me but she had cast on her foot at that time. I was out with Eileen Walch that time. She was here teaching school. It was falltime and some of us are getting to

Altona with her .22 Special, Ruby 1980. She split a half-inch thick willow about 50 feet away with this shot.

Altona with a beaver she trapped.

116

feel desperate because we can't get meat. Everytime we go hunting, nothing happens.

So we're out the road and I see moose on the hill. Pretty soon Eileen seen it. I told her, "Just go slow but don't idle your engine so it makes too much noise. Just make the same noise all the time." So I got out and got up on the back of the truck. I shot through it's ear and shot part of his horn too. Then I knocked and said to stop. I jumped off the truck and started walking on top of the hill at Twenty-five Mile. I run up little bit. I thought maybe I raised the gun too much. It's brand new .30-30 and the first time I ever shot it. When I got closer, I took shot at it in the head and there it fell. So he's got four bullets in him. Two shots in the ear, one in the horn and that last one. Here it stood broadways. Good target.

Papa used to say, "When you go hunting, when the meat, bear, anything turn around and stand broadways when you are following it, it's your meat. Don't quit it. Right there is your meat." How many times I used to cry. Come home over the hill, eighteen miles and the moose run away from me. On the snowshoes. I'm always on snowshoes. And they circle right around me and come back and stand where I started out from.

I fooled it one time over on Main Creek. I was setting my beaver trap and I see this moose run away. So I got on top of the bank and went home and got my .22 special. So I went down to where he first run away. As I was going down, he was coming off the hill. He made a big circle and was going to fool me but I waited till he come back. Just like I was playing a game those days. It was nothing for me to walk on snowshoes.

Nowadays there's truck, snow machine, or boat with kicker. It's so easy to get an animal on the road or river — people feel so proud. It's when snow is deep and you follow on showshoes because you're hungry that it's hard work. But I learned from Papa if moose goes straight ahead, don't follow it. It'll trick you and come back around. When it stands broadways, that's when it's yours.

Chapter Eight: Yuki Lake Alone

Tamarack My Friend

About six years ago something was bothering me. I know it was something besides my heart. I know when my heart is kicking up. So I went down to the store in Ruby and told Harold Esmailka, "Harold, I want you to take me down to Yuki Lake. I want to go down there and camp."

"Ha!" he says, "Who's going with you?"

I said, "Nobody."

"Are you okay?" he said.

"Sure I'm okay."

"Don't you feel well?" he ask me.

I said, "No and yes."

"Okay," he said, "I'll take you down there, but you don't want to stay too long. You have to be sure that you're alright."

I say, "Sure I'm alright. I just want to camp out." So I took six traps. Small traps for trapping muskrat under the ice. Then he hold me for a little while down at the plane before we take off.

He said, "You know, I don't like to take you down there. If the kids weren't going to school, we'd send them right down there."

I said, "No, I don't want no kids with me. I don't want nobody with me. I want to be alone." So I went.

It only took us twenty-five minutes to go down there. We flew around those lakes where I used to be and where the folks used to camp. I said, "Okay, go toward the Yukon." We circled around and I said, "That's the lake."

"You're really going to camp there?"

I said, "Yes." I took my tent, stove, gun, snowshoes, traps, food, chain-saw, and everything. I figured on staying two weeks. He helped me pack the stuff up the bank.

He said, "If I had time, I'd knock down this big pole for you."

I said, "Nope, you still have to go to Anchorage today. It's leaning, all I have to do is put my chainsaw on there and boom, it'll fall down. I'll have all kinds of wood right at the door of the tent. Nice dry wood." But he help me get poles for the tent and then say a few things before he left.

He had to go Outside to Washington but he said he'll be back to get me in a week. Then as he was going down to the lake to his airplane out on the ice, I said, "I'd like to spend two weeks here, Harold. All two weeks."

He holler back to me, "You got all your pills?" I told him I did. Then he said, Okay, I'll see you in two weeks."

So he took off. I knock down the tree. Sawed off a couple blocks. Nice big trees. Dry as a bone. Then I put up my tent. I built a fire first. A great big fire where I'm going to pitch the tent. There was still quite a bit of snow so I built that fire and melt it away. Pitch the tent, put all kind of spruce boughs in there. I put my stove in and burn up the nice wood right by the door.

Right in front of the tent was a big long lake. And across there was another lake. And way over was another big, big lake with beaver and few muskrat houses where people used to camp long ago. They called it *Totsidza Yeet*. I want to go across the lake. Well, soon as I get that tent all ready and stove going I made myself something to eat. I put the radio on, listen to the news, I ate. And by that time, I'm no good.

"This tent is in front of my cabin at Agate that fell in. I went to trap beaver because I needed a new boat. Then Zeta came along. 1953 maybe."

That was before the doctor took my gall bladder out, and whatever I eat don't agree with me. That's my big problem. Oh, those doctors put me through all kinds of tests. One time they think there was something in my stomach. They put that tube in there with lights and everything. Ohhh, that was terrible. And they didn't find nothing. so that's why I'm out there. I'm going to find out for myself. All they do is give me a lot of medication and they don't know what it is. And everything I eat made me sick.

I got up early the next morning and had a Cup of Soup and eat that for breakfast. If I eat in the middle of the day and walk it off I'm not too bad. So I start walking. Walk across to that beaver house. Walk to that muskrat house, putting traps in. I was so busy I didn't know the ducks came.

I started to cut down on my medicine this whole first week out there. I tapered down everyday and nothing happened. I felt real good. But just one spot was still bad. I said to myself, okay, take care of that one. I thought it was my liver because I can taste it almost. I could taste that bile. My food just tasted terrible. Otherwise I felt good. I had a good time out there.

One day I overdone it. I been out there eight days maybe. I went way out to a little creek. Coming back I was getting sick. And it was hard walking. Soft snow, deep, and my snowshoes got wet. I had a hard time walking through the slush. I went through the portage and I thought to myself, I wish some miracle happen, something funny where I'll be happy.

Well, I was walking, falling around. I was walking with a stick. Then I came to a bunch of trees, young trees. And I was falling around. And one tree look like three of them. It was going up and down and double vision. I thought, "Okay, old girl. You prepare yourself for where you'll sit. Let the mice eat you up."

I stop right there in between those trees and take off my packsack and gun, .22 Special. Those trees were little and soft enough to bend. They're only as high as the ceiling. So I bend them over toward me and made a nice place for myself. It was just like sitting on a chair. I looked at my time. It was around eleven o'clock. Then I must have passed out or went to sleep. Just laying against those trees like sitting in a rocking chair.

I didn't have enough energy to lift my head up and look up. I just laid back and went to sleep. How easy that would be. I prayed for my poor old soul. I thought I talked to Mom. When I know I'm very sick, I always call to her. It seems like she answers me. Or I just imagine she does. Oh my, I don't know how long I laid there.

All of a sudden I started waking up. I was cold. It was late in the evening. The sun was

Looking through the tamarack.

on my left side now and hitting me. I guess that's what woke me up. My face was just like wood, couldn't feel nothing. I try to move but I can only move my left leg little bit. I try to jump up but, no, couldn't even move. I laid back again. I don't know how long I slept again. This time I know I slept because I could hear these ducks and geese in my sleep going by to the lake.

When I woke up again, my legs were jumpy. It tingle when it started waking up. And my one hand was just like ice. I couldn't move it. So I get hold of the tree with my other hand and lift myself up. Then I put my hands on my knees and stoop over. I stand that way for a few minutes. I don't dare sit back in that place. I see my snowshoes is dry now and I looked at the time. It was 6:15.

I talk to myself, "Okay, you get home or you'll lay down here and let the mice eat you up." I kneel down on my snowshoes and cut one of those trees. Just big enough for my cane. I never see what it was. I was dopey anyway. I couldn't see straight. And here it was tamarack. A bunch of tamarack. And nowhere near there isn't any. I already cut it. So I was talking to it. I said,

goodies. Like spruce gum, just the right kind that turn pink when you chew it. It's not bitter. Gee, it's good.

After dinner the sun was still up so I went back down again. I took the four traps and put it on long willow, all four of them. Set it right on the edge of the water, in shallow water. I went home. I talk to myself, "Well, I'll have ducks tomorrow, whole bunch." That's what I was fooling around with from there on until about four or five days later. The snow had gone, most of it. Ice was melting.

Muskrat opened up the holes again so I took those traps away from the ducks. I didn't want that many ducks. I had to wade out there in the water to get them. The snowmachine boots get full of water. Just having a great time. I put two traps in the hole for muskrat and I left two down there to catch geese.

One day I come out and hear this funny noise, just like pulling a cork out of a bottle. You know, it makes big noise. I was wondering what in the world is that. I went over to the portage and thousands and thousands of cranes land right in front of me. Ah, what a beautiful sound. And after they light, they dance.

They're dancing away and I holler at them and sing to them. Same with the geese and ducks. Praise it. Talk to it in Indian. "Let everybody be well and feed upon you." Indians used to always talk to the first ducks, geese or anything that comes in. They were so hungry. They praise it so that people would enjoy them and be well in the summertime.

This one time I went back there in the afternoon. Here was great big thing! White, look like a bunch of snow or foam out there on the water. I started to look at it. It's not very far, but how you going to get it? I don't know how to swim. And then, ahh, he put out his head. It was two swan! It was like a big ball out there with his head down in the bottom of the lake. And when they pull it out, God, beautiful.

Like a crazy fool, I went back to the tent and got the gun. I was just aiming it. I could have killed it, nothing would stop me. All of a sudden I thought, what am I going to do with it if I kill it? I scold myself. They were so beautiful and I almost killed it. I know I wasn't supposed to . Oh my, $500 fine. People used to eat it. I know my brother killed one there long ago. Then I put my gun up and take the shell out. That swan put up his neck and make that noise. He never flied away. I start talking to him and everything.

The next day Harold came. I was way down messing with my traps. I hear him buzzing. He circled the camp and then he must have seen my trail. He come right on top of me just like! Barooommm! Then he buzz all the ducks and it looked like the whole lake was coming up. Gosh, he had more fun. Finally I took the traps and started walking back. He landed right on the lake and came to meet me.

"You really got tan. Now you look like an Indian," he said.

I said, "Harold, I thank God that you brought me down."

"Well," he said, "what did you find out?"

"Harold, I got to go to hispital. I'm tired of being sick anyway."

In no time at all we pick up that camp, pack up and put everything in the plane. I said, "Oh, why don't you let me stay? You can bring me boat."

"You come on home," he said. "You had everybody jumping on me about letting that old lady go down there. Oh, old lady I tell them, you people are more old lady than she is."

Anyway, everyday or every other day he had his fliers in Galena buzzing my camp. He told them to watch out for me down there. They'd see me at home or out monkeying with the ducks. And my grandson, Claude, came to visit me one night with one of the Farmer boys. It was a beautiful two weeks time. If I had snowmachine I would have gone everywhere when it turned cold. I had a good time.

Well, he brought me home to Ruby. We landed on the river with skis. It was still ice but shore water running by the bank so they had to bring me in from the plane by boat. Harold left his plane there and right away took off for Anchorage or Fairbanks from the airfield. He was gone about five days.

Everyone got concerned about the airplane out there on the ice. Water started running on the edge and the shore ice was caving in. We were all talking about it and I wanted to know if one of his fliers could go down there and fly it up to the field.

Harold Esmailka in front of his store making radio contact with one of his pilots. March 1979.

Ruby from the cemetary hill, 1980.

125

But it had skis on and there was no snow up there. Just as we're all talking about it here comes his plane. Everybody got excited. He brought the wheels down from the field, throw it in the boat and went out there and put the wheels on the airplane. This was about two o'clock when they finish.

I forgot now what day in May it was. It was late. The Nenana had gone already. So he took off. The boys came back to shore with skis and pulled the boat up. Harold land his plane up at the field and just as he was coming back to town, somebody said, "Ice is going! There goes the ice!" It waited for him. That close. My, I even went to see him. He came over, put his arm around me, hug me, and said, "Okay, how about that?"

I said, "That's us. that's okay!"

Well, I didn't go to the hospital till last part of June. I had to have my garden all planted first. That was six years ago. I had to go back in July to have my pacemaker changed. I just wear these things out in eighteen months and have to change it everytime. Four years later I had an attack and that's when they took out my gall bladder. Oh, I'm in and out of that hospital but I got to keep busy. Have to have my garden. And winter-time, now I have my own sno-go. But I still have to walk on my snowshoes. My snowshoes and me are good friends.

Altona's grandson, Claude Keough sitting in her garden in Ruby.

126

Index

adoption 16,29,112
airplane 108,125,126
alcohol (see liquor)
Anchorage 73
Antoski, Lincoln 33
bear 33,34,61,69-83,113-116
beaver 73,100
berrypicking 114
Bettles 14
Big Albert 14
Big Joe 12-17,21-36,39-45,48,54-65,
    69-89,95-97,102,104
Big Joe, Emily 24-37,39-41,48,54-67,
    84-91,104
Big Joe, Rocker 33,92
Big Joe, Thomas 28,33,38,53-57,63,69,70
Bishop Mountain 39
Bishop Seghers 39
Bogie, Grandma 21-23
Brown, Alexander Sr. (see "Dago Kid")
Brown, Alexander "Buster" 98,104
building (also, see houses)
Burk, Billy Sr. 63,89,102,103
Burk, Rose (Big Joe) 16,38-41,53,60,63,
    88-91
camp 69,76-83,115,118-125
Carey, Jack 38
caribou 13,14,48
Catholic (Mission) 63
Chena 16
chicken (grouse) 104,105
childbirth 16,19,20,27,28,41,62,98,99
childcare 17,41,42,111,112
children (also, see young people) 12
Circle 16
clothing 14,46,69
cold 48
communication 45,46,70
Cripple 73
cutting wood (see wood)
"Dago Kid" 68,84-110
dancing 21,105-107
Dawson 16
Dayton, Albert 73-75
Dean, Mary 13
death 21,41-43,49-59,63,66,109,110
Devane, Tom 39,84-88,108

Dodson, Jim 109
dogs 12,92-94,102,105
Dolbi 12,44
drowning 63
ducks 123-125
economics (storekeeping, wages...) 32,
    92-96,108,113
education 38-40,95
Eight Mile 32-34,38,60
epidemic 52-56
Esmailka, Harold 27,118,119,125,126
Fairbanks 109,110
fire 103
fishing (fishwheel, fishcamp, fishtrap) 17,
    18,29-32,94-98,115
Flat 94,105
food 21-23,33,34,40,48-52,71-83,103-105,
    117
Fourth of July 105,106
frogs 36,37
Galena 28,67,73,110,125
gambling 97,105-109
games 53
geese 123-125
goldmining 9,14,15,24-26,32,60,105-107
grandma 41,42,53,58,59,61
Gurtler 18,19
Hardluck, Ivan 85,86
healthcare 27,28,54-57,68,118-126
Henry Haemon 28
Hoffman, Anne 84,85
Holy Cross 112
horses 105
houses 91
Hunter, Marie 33,68,89,99,102,110-112
hunting 13,14,34,48-52,57,70-83,104,109,
    113-117
hutIanee 26,34,61,69-71,76-83
Iditarod 94
Innoko 9
Jette, Father 35,57,62
Jimmy, Rebecca 76
Kateel 12,44,74
Keough, Claude 33,111,125,126
Kk'okkanaa 12-14
Kokrines 16,48,58,60-62,66,84-86
Koyukuk 38

Koyukuk River 14,44
language (also, see Koyukon) 5,33,85
Lewis, Dave 24-27
Lewis Landing 23-26
liquor 32,47
Long Creek 105-107
Louden 13,21-23,28,33,35,38,41
luck 70
mail 93
Marie, Jan 24,28
Marie, Tom 28
marriage 12-16,60-66,84-91
marshalls 93
McGrath 92-94
McKinley Park 92-94
McCormick, Miss 38
medicine people 17,29,34-37,43-47,49-52,
    62,84
Melozi Station 32,39,56
Melozitna River 32
men 69-73
missionaries 34,35,39
moose 34,116,117
muskrat 118
names 42,43
Natives 38,45-47
Nenana 33,103
Noosa Ghunh 23-26
Notti, Madeline 67,88
Novi River 16
Nulato 16,33,38,58
old ways (beliefs) 61,77,82,83
Ophir 92,99-102
Pearl 110,112
polio 38,39,53-59
Poorman 105-107
potlatch 12,21-23,61
ratting (see muskrat)
roadhouse 24-26,111
Ross, Doc 67
Rossi, Father 35,57
Ruby 26-31,38,44-47,54,84-92,102,103,118
sailing 17
school (also, see education) 38,111
Seattle 102,103
sewing 113,114
shaman (see medicine people)

shelter (see houses) 12,13
Slaveenga, John 60-68
snowshoes 121,126
Solomon, Herbert 73-83
Solomon, Madeline 16,43,73-83
Sophia 103
songs 21
spring (camp & activities) 84,118-126
sports 12
starvation 48
steamboats 14,25,32,44-47
Stickman, Old Man 16,28,29
story telling 18,37,40
suicide 112,
Sulatna 48,104,105
taboos (see hutIanee)
tamarack 55,56,118-121
Tanana 12,42,58,62
telegraph 32
Toby, Johnson 74-80
tools 13
trading 13,14,45-47
transportation 48,61,74,92-94,102,103
trapping 20,21,33,73-83,99-107,109,124
travel 12,24-26,73-83
Walsh, Eileen 116-117
Walker, Johnny 105
Whiskey Creek 17
White (people) 32,38,44-47
Williams, Cecelia & Uncle 16
women 12-21,35,69-83,113
wood 105,
working for wages 91-94,110-113
young people (also, see children) 112
Yrjana, Dolly 114-116
Yuki River 23,32,118-125
Yukon River 95

Altona Brown Family Tree

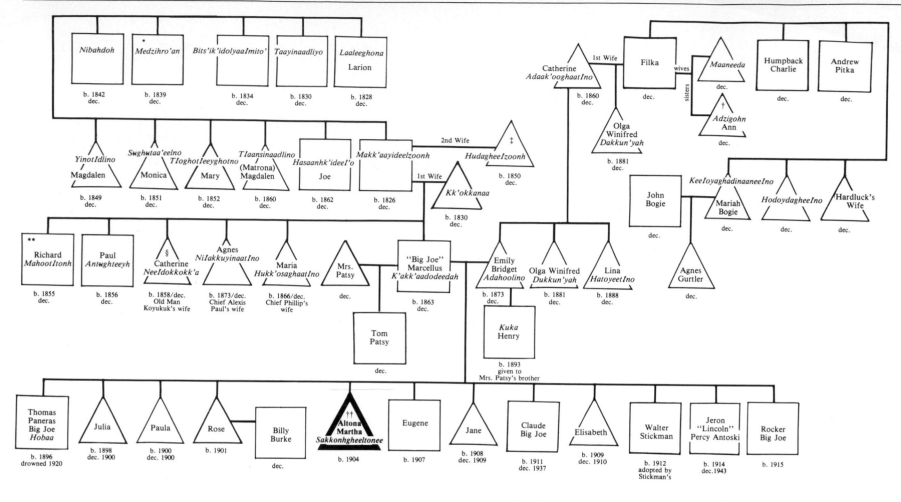

Legend

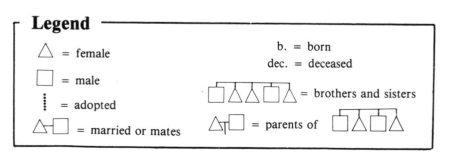

△ = female
□ = male
⋮ = adopted
△—□ = married or mates

b. = born
dec. = deceased
□△△△△ = brothers and sisters
△□ = parents of □△△△

* Jette's spelling with old Koyukon orthography.
† Raised Altona's mother, Emily.
‡ Big Joe's half sisters from Makk'aayideelzooh and Hudagheeɬzoonh were *Niɬtoryere'Inol* (Susie), *Kanorodala*, *MetorodtIno* (Sophie). (Jette's orthography)
§ Her first husband was Pitka.
** Married to *Kk'ohɨnaa'oh*, Cheechako John's mother.
†† Altona thought her baptized name was Marie but according to church records it's Martha.

128